Reflections From the Road

BY JIM REA

DEDICATION

This book is dedicated to the memory of my grandparents, Davy and Mary McCaughrin, and of my parents Billy and Peggy Rea, all now a long time in the Father's House.

Also to the memory of the Reverend Noel Agnew, former minister of West Kirk Presbyterian Church, Shankill Road, with whom I shared ministry in 2006 - 2009. Noel was called home 30.9.20 as I wrote the final lines of this book. Noel brought the' Gospel to the Road.'

Some names have been changed to protect anonymity.

Scripture quotations are taken from the Holy Bible,
New International Version, © 1973, or New Living Translation, © 1996.

Author can be contacted at wjimrea@gmail.com

All proceeds from the sale of this book
after production and distribution costs will be donated to the Welcome Organisation,
The Salvation Army and East Belfast Mission's Hosford House (charities for the homeless).

DESIGN • PRINT • PUBLISHING • DISTRIBUTION

CEDRIC WILSON

Designed & Published by Cedric Wilson
Email: cedricwilson@live.co.uk

FOREWORD

It was probably in the mid seventies when I first met the Reverend Jim Rea. I was then in my late teens, cautiously exploring faith, and Jim was the minister in Irvinestown and Pettigo Methodist churches. Jim hosted a week of youth events in Pettigo Methodist church hall and as a result of the impact of that week, listening to Jim's preaching and a series of things that came together, I came to a place of real faith and commitment to Christ. In the months that followed I attended services on Sunday evenings in that circuit, was encouraged in those early months as a new Christian by Jim's warm and thoroughly biblical teaching, and for some years was a member of Pettigo Christian Endeavour where I continued to be nurtured as a young follower of Jesus.

Years later in 2001 I arrived in east Belfast as the rector of Willowfield. I kept meeting people who told stories of Jim's leadership and ministry in the Newtownards Road East Belfast Methodist mission. There were stories of lives changed, people being brought to faith, and the love of Jesus being demonstrated in practical ways.

Jim's evangelical preaching, his strong leadership, his compassion for people, especially those overlooked by others, his visionary courage and creative risk-taking, and all for the sake of making Christ known, are qualities that the church in Ireland desperately needs today. I still meet people in east Belfast and beyond who thank God, as I do, for the work and ministry of Jim Rea.

Jim has that unusual ability to put people at ease, to make you feel valued while at the same time challenging you to live a life of uncompromising faith in Christ and obedience to Christ. When I was asked earlier this year, prior to my consecration as bishop, if there was one of the past presidents of the Methodist church that I would like as one of the consecrating bishops I did not have to pause for thought, and immediately asked that it would be the Reverend Jim Rea.

I have so enjoyed reading the stories that Jim tells in this book. Jim has blessed so many lives and while these are stories of the grace of God at work in the lives of men and women, this same grace that used Jim Rea to strengthen, encourage and equip God's people in this book will use you and me to carry God's grace to those around us. The Gospel that the stories in this book bear testimony to is still the power of God to change lives today.

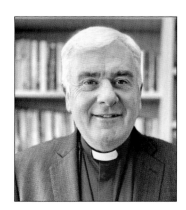

The Right Reverend David A McClay,
Bishop of Down and Dromore

ABOUT THE AUTHOR

Celebrating our 50th outside under lockdown

Jim Rea is a retired Methodist minister. He was elected President of the Methodist Church in Ireland in 2003. He worked on the Newtownards Road in Belfast at the Methodist Church for twenty one years and in 1985 founded the East Belfast Mission.

In 1995 he was awarded an MBE for services to the community. Jim has witnessed some of the most horrific events of the troubles in Northern Ireland and his ministry has been almost exclusively in areas of conflict where he has ministered to many victims. Attempting to bring an end to violence he engaged with the leadership of opposing paramilitary organisations. In 1999 he was stationed in Portadown and was involved in mediation to diffuse the impass at Drumcree. In 2006 he came back to work at the Methodist Church on the Shankill Road. He has a strong pastoral commitment to people with addictions. He has travelled widely as a preacher and evangelist and is a regular contributor on BBC Radio Ulster's 'Thought for the Day', and Downtown Radio's, 'Just a Moment'. He also contributes to a religious column in the Belfast Newsletter.

Jim is married to Carol, they have three married children and six grandchildren.

INTRODUCTION

I never considered that after writing 'Stories from the Streets' I would produce a sequel, but the success and encouragement I got from this publication was beyond all expectation. The profits from the book have allowed me to contribute a total of £10K to the Welcome Organisation and East Belfast Mission's Hosford House, both charities for the homeless. The residue of profit, alongside support from the Irish Temperance League, has enabled this publication.

I also want to thank a number of sponsors of 'Stories from the Streets' who created the access to funds that made its publication possible. This also enabled me to give free copies to Northern Ireland's public libraries, the prison libraries, and other public places such as waiting rooms, as well as using discretion to give some people the book as a gift. Also several well-known politicians, north and south, have expressed their appreciation at receiving a copy. People who have read the book have contacted me from different parts of the world to express appreciation.

The idea of this sequel 'Reflections from the Road' came on the eve of lockdown due to Covid-19. Being unable to leave home focused my concentration on writing.

My central purpose in writing these two books is to share the truths of the Gospel through these true stories, and also to honour the memory of some remarkable people I have met, some of them well-known and some hardly known at all. My aim will have been achieved if the stories help readers realise what it means to follow Jesus and experience the greatest hope of all: the wonder of a life that never ends and continues in the new heaven and the new earth, where there will be no sorrow, sadness or pandemics.

Rev Jim Rea
*Former President of the
Methodist Church.*

CONTENTS

CONTENTS

YOU NEVER KNOW HOW THINGS END UP

Jack Smyth

I could never have believed that a single meeting would change my ultimate direction in life. My grandfather had a niece called Barbara who was married to Bob Smyth and they had three sons, Bobby, George and Jack. My grandparents greatly admired these three boys and often spoke affectionately about them. However, I never really knew them well and was only acquainted from a distance.

It was in the early 1960s that I first made my way to Shankill Methodist Church. It came about in a rather strange set of circumstances.

One night while walking up the Woodvale Road I met Jack Smyth and we had a short conversation, after which he invited me to Shankill Methodist. He said, "I will meet you outside the church on Sunday and bring you into the service," and true to his word he did, and we went in together. Encouraged by Jack I continued to attend Shankill Methodist Church and became involved in the Christian Endeavour Society, the Sunday night fellowship and several other activities. I had earlier been converted to faith in Jesus Christ at the age of 14. In Shankill Methodist I found fellowship and friends - one being a young woman called Carol, who was to become my wife. While there were many

Old Shankill Church

other people who had a great influence on my call to the ministry, I will never forget Jack Smyth.

Jack eventually became a Methodist Local Preacher. He had a deep conviction about his beliefs and would hold his corner in any discussion but he was a modest and gracious man. Every time we met he offered words of encouragement and would ask with great interest about what was happening in the church where I was serving. Above all he would want to hear about people being converted to Christ.

In 2003 when I was installed as President of the Methodist Church I recall thinking, as I saw Jack with his wife Sandra in the congregation, would I be here tonight if Jack had not met me at the door outside the church that Sunday morning, a day I cannot even place a date on? In May 2004, before my year as President ended, Jack died after a short illness. In the last days of his life he radiated confidence. He would share the great Salvation Army declaration that he was being "promoted to Glory." I was privileged to tell this story at his funeral service. His lasting memory for me will be that a simple act of friendship, in the providence of God, can have a lasting legacy.

DON'T GO TO THE DOCTOR BEFORE YOU SEE SAM

Sam Wright

Sam owned a chemist's shop on the lower Newtownards Road in east Belfast, where he had become a household name. "Go and see Sam," the locals would say, if someone felt unwell or needed a bit of advice. I too greatly admired Sam and took his medical advice on many occasions, especially his homespun cures for minor ailments.

Sam was always pleasant and helpful to every customer. As I got to know him better he would invite me in behind the counter into his dispensary for a short conversation, and often he offered me a word of encouragement. One day in the dispensary I noticed that he was doing a difficult job, bandaging the ulcerated leg of an elderly man, whom I knew to have serious alcohol problems and who lived in terrible housing conditions. Even though Sam's shop had a pleasant aroma from the perfumes and the soaps, on this occasion I was almost knocked out by the awful smell coming from the old man's leg. Bending down as he bandaged the leg, Sam did the task with a smile. It was typical of the man, who treated everyone alike and offered practical help whatever the circumstances.

A few days later I had reason to return to Sam's shop. I thought I would speak to Sam about what I had observed him doing. "Sam," I said, "I really admire the way you treat people and especially the way in which you gave time and help to that old guy whose leg was so smelly." Sam looked at me and smiled, "Well Jim, it is like this, I don't consider myself better than anyone else; I am simply a sinner saved by grace," and then he paused and remarked, "On the other hand neither is anyone better than I am, for I am a child of the King."

Come to think of it, Sam was just echoing words from Paul's letter to the Ephesians,

"It is by grace you have been saved and God raised us up with Christ and seated us with him in the heavenly realms in Christ Jesus, in order that in the coming ages he might show the incomparable riches of his grace, expressed in his kindness to us in Christ Jesus. For it is by grace you have been saved, through faith—and this not from yourselves, it is the gift of God—not by works, so that no one can boast. For we are God's workmanship, created in Christ Jesus to do good works, which God prepared in advance for us to do." Ephesians 2:5-10 NIV

SAINTS AND SINNERS IN LIGONIEL

On the buses

The Ligoniel /Ballysillan area of north Belfast where I grew up was full of characters. There was Sammy Heaney, known as the Lord Mayor of Ligoniel. Sammy liked a liquid lunch and would often enter churches somewhat inebriated, offering a different tune to the singing. No one ever asked Sammy to leave, people accepted him as he was. Then there was John who had his trousers tied up with a rope and was always up for free buns and tea if the opportunity arose.

In contrast, there was Billy Cathcart the bus inspector who ran the bus like an army camp, instructing hangers-on on the platform that there were seats upstairs. He had some understanding of health and safety and would never let the bus overflow with passengers. I don't know how he would have coped with Belfast's Glider packed like herrings in a barrel. Billy also led the singing at the mission hall on Ligoniel Road. It had its many homespun theologians like Sammy Patterson and Sammy Morrison. They were all part of the Sunday School I attended for a time. The Sunday School exam was something else. You learnt a passage of scripture and on examination day, the two Sammys sat at the back of the room while your Sunday School teacher asked you questions. These two professors then gave you a

mark that decided whether you got a special prize, a leather-bound copy of the Authorised Version, or one with a less stylish binding.

Clara Kennedy was probably the first saint I ever met. This was not what I personally concluded, but how the locals described this lady in and around Ligoniel and Ballysillan. I was only 12 years old when I first met her. My recollections are of a plain looking, quiet spoken lady with a radiant smile. Clara worked

Sammy Patterson and Sammy Morrison Mission Hall Ligoniel

hard in one of the local linen mills in Ligoniel. She lived in a modest little home and shared what she had with others, albeit she didn't have much but she had a radiant smile and an open house to anyone who called.

There was much concern in the community when she became unwell, and was diagnosed with something that appeared life threatening and sinister. People on "our side of the house," as we say, talked in whispers albeit not demeaningly, of the people in the nearby St Vincent de Paul's Catholic Church who were lighting candles for her. It was a mark of the respect in which she was held by everyone in the days preceding the Troubles in this mixed and friendly community. What was more amazing was her recovery and the common view that God had healed her. She lived for many more years and continued to work in the local Elim Pentecostal Church in many different ways. What was so attractive about her was her consistent Christian witness and the natural way in which she talked about her love for Jesus Christ. She was never condescending or judgmental, but expressed her faith with great humility.

On November the 1st, All Saints Day, many of us give thanks to God for those incredible people who have had an impact on our lives and are now in heaven with their Lord. Over the years I have had to refine my thinking about who the saints really are. Some of us put the saints in stained glass windows, pray to them for special favours or just see them as extraordinary Christians; the New Testament offers a different perspective. Paul refers to the Christians in one city as "the saints who are at Philippi". In the New Testament the Greek word hagios (literally meaning 'holy') is used of God's people and is translated as 'saints' meaning 'holy ones.' This really means to be 'set apart', and the holiness of the saints is then the conduct expected of every Christian who is separated or set apart unto God. The truth is that every believer who seeks to put Jesus Christ at the centre of his or her life is a saint, even though they wouldn't have the presumption to claim it.

That is what Clara, Billy and the two Sammys were. They never would have claimed to be saints, but in reality they were.

SEE YOU NEXT YEAR REVEREND

I only began to appreciate the importance of Harvest when I became a minister in rural Fermanagh in the early 1970s. The Harvest services attracted the largest congregations of the year, even outdoing the great Christian festivals of Christmas and Easter. Indeed, for many the Harvest was the only service they attended during the year. One such was Lily, a woman with a sharp turn of phrase and a great sense of humour. "I'll see you at the Harvest," she said to me one day when I was visiting her home. True to her word, I spotted her sitting halfway down the church and made sure to shake her hand as she left the service. I still remember it vividly: she looked straight at me and with a twinkle in her eye remarked, "I will see you next year, Reverend."

After further visits to Lily's home, I was soon to become aware of the reason for her once a year attendance. "I am as good as many of the people that go to that church," she would say, "and you don't need to go to church to be a Christian." With that I would heartily agree, but tried to explain that church-going by itself is not the way by which we are accepted by God, rather it is our acceptance of the unconditional love of God shown in Jesus Christ that is central to being a Christian. However, I was never sure at the time whether Lily with all her frankness and humour quite understood that. What I was to discover was that such views were not uncommon; I have heard them expressed on countless occasions.

I am reminded that the service Lily attended annually is called the Harvest Thanksgiving, the emphasis being on thanksgiving with particular reference to the material provisions God gives to us. Early Christians met on the first day of the week to celebrate the risen Lord and to worship, pray and listen to the apostles' teaching. That's what we do every Sunday, Harvest or otherwise, whether searchers, seekers or believers. I think that if Lily ever discovered what I tried to share with her in that farmhouse kitchen she might have said, "See you next week, Reverend."

A GLIMMER OF HOPE

George Bush

In the winter of 1982 George Bush, then American Vice President, represented the U.S. at the funeral of the former Soviet leader Leonid Brezhnev. He was deeply moved by a silent action carried out by Brezhnev's widow Viktoria. This was the old Soviet Union ruled by atheistic communism. Many Christians worshipped secretly, fearing imprisonment. Any outward expression of faith was likely to bring at the very least an expression of anger from the authorities, and would be especially frowned on if it came from a public figure.

George Bush watched Viktoria's expression of grief with interest. She stood motionless by the coffin until seconds before it was closed. Then, just as the soldiers touched the lid to put it in place, Brezhnev's widow performed an act of great courage and hope, a gesture that would have been unacceptable in that culture: she reached down and made the sign of the cross on her husband's chest. This bereaved woman hoped there was another life, and that that life was best represented

Viktoria and Leonid Brezhnev

by Jesus who died on the cross. On that sad day the hope of the good news of resurrection was making its witness in unfamiliar surroundings.

The message of the resurrection of Jesus Christ continues to speak to us. It is the central hope of the Christian faith, hope that death will be overcome and life everlasting will be the experience of all who believe. Much evidence supports it, the records of the

four gospel writers and the witnesses to the event. Their despondency is transformed into exuberant joy. Many leading scholars have researched the evidence only to come to the conclusion that Jesus Christ has been raised from the dead.

I pray that with even greater confidence we will be able to say, as some do in their church liturgies, "Dying you destroyed our death. Rising you restored our life. Lord Jesus, come in glory."

Red Square

A VERY RICH WOMAN

It was another Wednesday at the senior citizens' meeting at the East Belfast Mission. I looked around, there was no pianist. Without a pianist our singing would never match the Plymouth Brethren or the Reformed Presbyterians who can sing without accompaniment and make a fair job of it. At the best of times our senior citizens sounded like the cats' choir with a few dogs thrown in.

Suddenly a lady appeared at the door. I had never seen her before. So I asked the question again, "Anybody to play the piano?" Suddenly this stranger stood up, and soon we were singing "Count your many blessings, name them one by one, and it will surprise you what the Lord has done." Well, at least we had got somebody to play, although this lady played in the rhythm of what I call the pub pianist.

East Belfast Mission

This was her introduction to the East Belfast Mission, where she was to become a regular. I would often meet her in our day centre and we would talk. Sarah was very wise; she had experienced the trials and tribulations of life through poverty. Widowed early in life, she brought up a large family. For years she lived close to the lough shore in Sydenham and told me that she would send her children to the shore to pick up pieces of coal that had fallen off the coal boats going into the Belfast Harbour. This was the only way she could heat her home. Above all she would say that she wished for nothing and had learned to trust the Lord for every day. Over the years I got to know a lot about Sarah. I guess at the time she was in her sixties.

One day, having shared accommodation with family, she decided she would move on. It was a Sunday afternoon when she called at our manse

in the leafy suburbs of east Belfast. "I am moving on," she said. "Oh," I said, "can I help you to move your stuff?" "No, everything I own is in there," she answered and pointed to two black bin bags. Then she explained. "Owning things only complicates your life. I don't want stuff, and you can take none of it with you."

Some time later, after a short illness, Sarah died. As I reflect I recall some of the world's richest people: the football divas, the oil magnates, the property giants. Then I think of Sarah. Materially she had virtually nothing, but she knew where her real inheritance lay and was truly rich, having discovered the reality of those wonderful words of St Paul:

2 Corinthians 8:9 New International Version (NIV)
> *For you know the grace of our Lord Jesus Christ, that though he was rich, yet for your sake he became poor, so that you through his poverty might become rich.*

NO SURRENDER

Ibrox Stadium

One day the funeral director called me and asked me to conduct a funeral of a man called Alan Short. As always I would talk to the family to get to know something about the deceased.

When I arrived at the home I was told I should refer to the deceased as Shortie even though he was six foot three. It was also important to mention his fanatical support for Rangers Football Club. They went on to tell me that he was a dedicated member of a South Belfast Loyalist Flute Band, and I was assured most of the band would

South Belfast flute band

attend. I took copious notes, hoping that I could do my best at the funeral at Roselawn Crematorium. I got the impression that Shortie was a big character who had an influence for good on the band.

When we got to the crematorium a young man with a strong Glaswegian accent approached me, introducing himself as Brian. He said he would like to say a word about Shortie on behalf of the band. "I will say nothing to offend you, Reverend, in fact, I will quote scripture." So I agreed. When I invited Brian to speak, some of his reflections on Shortie brought laughter. And then, true to his word, it came: "Shortie always told me that the Rangers were mentioned in the Bible. Psalm 95 verse 7

WE ARE THE PEOPLE the sheep of his pasture.

I couldn't help but smile. "We are the people" is commonly used by Rangers fans (the Gers) to express their supremacy. Not so terribly relevant in recent years!

Then I had to speak. "Thanks Brian, what a great play on words." I then told the large number gathered that I wanted to speak on the words "No surrender." Suddenly I had a captive audience eating out of my hand. I paused and then went on. "I spell it differently. I spell it as K-N-O-W surrender." And I explained that the most important thing they could do was to surrender their lives to Jesus Christ. I explained how they might take that step. One wee man going out shook my hand warmly and said it was the best funeral he had ever been at, a bit over the top I thought. However I don't know of the long term impact, but I still pray that God may use those words, rather impromptu, or as they say in these parts, "on the hoof."

LACKING EXPECTATION

In 1970 I left Edgehill College to be sent to Cregagh Methodist Church, as what was then called in Methodism, a Junior Minister. If you are from other traditions, putting it simply I was the equivalent of an assistant or a curate. I found it all rather daunting as my boss was a big figure in Methodism at the time. The Rev Dr Hedley Washington Plunkett - Dr Plunkett as I referred to him - maintained he could trace his ancestry back to the Blessed Oliver Plunkett, now Saint Oliver as canonised by Pope Francis in 2018. Hedley Plunkett had a distinctive and colourful Fermanagh accent, and was engaging as a preacher.

Rev Dr Hedley Plunkett

Hedley was for a time the Methodist Church's evangelist, and during those years would travel throughout Ireland where he led many to a living faith. He then became the minister of Belfast Methodism's "cathedrals" at Carlisle Memorial and Donegall Square, both now closed. Now he was the minister at Cregagh Methodist, a church then with a large morning congregation of well over four hundred. He had a great work ethic, rising early in the morning to do some gardening, he would then spend some time in his study, and every afternoon would leave his manse to knock the doors of his congregation with its eleven hundred households. This was shared with me and a retired minister, the Rev Moore Graham, whose son and grandson Winston and Laurence would later become presidents of the Methodist Church, as did Hedley Plunkett in 1975.

It is only in recent years that looking back, I appreciate the influence he had upon me. Hedley was proud of his honorary doctorate and certainly not slow in his opinions of the church in his generation. Most people referred to him as Dr Plunkett, which I did until I became President of the Methodist Church and considered I could now throw caution to the wind and call him Hedley.

Reflecting on fifty years ago, memories of this man's influence still remain. He played an important part in my formation as a minister. On March 20th 1972, seven people were killed in a Provisional IRA bombing in Donegall Street, Belfast; one of those men had a link with Cregagh Methodist Church and I shared in the funeral service. I recall going to see this devastated family, and then there was the funeral. The understanding, love and tenderness with which Hedley conducted that service will never leave me; it was a dark day but God was there.

In 1971 Dr Martyn Lloyd-Jones came to Belfast to preach in the Wellington Hall and I went with my boss to hear him. Lloyd-Jones was an incredible preacher, regarded as the best Bible expositor in the United Kingdom. He preached that evening for around fifty minutes, which sounded like five. His text was from Romans 8 v 18: "For I reckon that the sufferings of this present time are not worthy to be compared with the glory which shall be revealed in us."

We both felt very uplifted by what we had heard. However, one minister perhaps not sympathetic to Lloyd-Jones turned around and remarked, "Do you know he quoted the text forty-two times?" I wasn't sure of his accuracy. Leaving the building Hedley whispered in my ear, "Don't listen to him Jim, he's only a crank." It made me laugh at his candour.

Leaving Cregagh to take up an appointment, I recall his splendid advice: "Never fight with people in your congregation about something petty. If it is an issue of doctrinal importance that is different. Sometimes ministers bring problems on themselves when the issue is of little importance in the grand scheme of things."

The last I would see of Hedley Plunkett was in a south Belfast nursing home where he spent his last days. He had dementia, but could carry on a sort of conversation. He was keen that I would get one message about the church he loved and served. "We lack expectation," he reminded me several times. Could he be right that the church in general lacks the anticipation, the expectation of what God can do? Despite his confusion, I believe his perception was not far off the mark.

Cregagh Methodist Church

THANKS IT'S WONDERFUL

Connolly Station Dublin

I still remember the day I sat on a virtually empty train at Connolly Station. Just before departure to Belfast the train filled up and a young African woman decided for some reason to sit opposite me. I wondered if she thought that I had a friendly face, as there were other seats available. Sitting down, she proceeded to lay out on our shared table her substantial lunch. I could soon realise by its aroma that it was

not tempting to my taste buds. After she finished, I asked her, "And where are you going today?" She then told me that she lived in Drogheda but worked in Dublin. She was one of what we now call "the new Irish." I soon gained from her conversation that she was struggling to make a living with housing costs, part of the reason for living out of Dublin. Ireland was far and above what life was like in Nigeria but it still wasn't easy.

Soon a Christian book I was reading caught her eye and this led to a conversation; she told me she was part of an emerging Pentecostal Church in Drogheda. As we chatted she soon discovered my calling in life. She then asked me about the different translations of the Bible in English. Do you have a Bible? I asked. "Yes, I have one, but it is old and in bad condition." I assured her that when I would get home I would send her a copy of the Bible. She was a most outgoing and lovely young woman.

Always keeping a few Bibles at home for such purposes, I found a modern translation and posted it to an address in Drogheda. Some weeks passed, when the phone rang, and it was from a pay phone - I knew as I heard coins dropping into the coin box at the instructions of the operator. It was the Nigerian lady. "Thank you for the Bible. It is wonderful." The conversation continued and then the call ended abruptly. Her money had run out. I never heard from her again.

Thumbing through a book recently I saw a quote from the famous 19th century preacher C.H. Spurgeon: "A Bible that's falling apart usually belongs to someone who isn't."

I thought of my African friend.

LOOKS ARE ONLY SKIN DEEP

Musgrave Park Hospital

I have always enjoyed broadcasting on radio and for many years I have recorded for Radio Ulster's Thought for the Day, and Downtown's Just a Moment. Some people who have never seen me, when I meet them casually will remark, "Oh I know who you are, I hear you on the radio, I recognise your voice. You're Jim Rea." I warmly acknowledge and am flattered by my slight call to fame.

Many years ago I was visiting a lady in Musgrave Park Hospital, Belfast. The patient in the next bed looked me up and down and then said in a very broad Belfast accent, "Are you Jim Rea?" "Yes that's me," I replied. "Oh," she says, "I hear ye on the radio, yer great, never miss ye." By such time my ego was swelling and I was inviting more compliments. But then I remembered I should give some pastoral attention to the lady I was visiting. Greeting both women on leaving, as I shook hands with my radio fan she looked me up and down, paused and then remarked, "Ye know somethin', ye sound better than ye luk." With a somewhat deflated ego I left the hospital but have often dined out on the story.

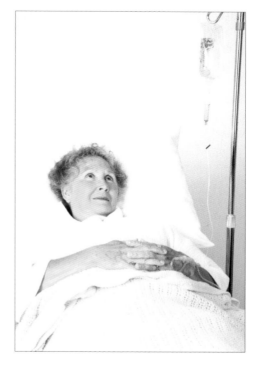

Looks are of course so important to many people. The glamour trade will do all they can to take your money and make you look better. So I am not condemning anyone for trying to look their best. It is a great boost to self esteem. And as I know, the ageing

26

process can't be avoided. I often wonder what the woman in the hospital would say now if she saw me. A telling verse in the Old Testament Book of Samuel, on the choice of David as King of Israel against other rivals, says: 'But the LORD said to Samuel, "The LORD does not look at the things people look at. People look at the outward appearance, but the LORD looks at the heart."'

As I reflect on this I recall that over my lifetime I have probably conducted over six hundred funerals. I reckon I have never said much about the deceased's appearance in life, perhaps occasionally a remark about their style. The stranger attending who has never seen the deceased, and comes as a friend or work colleague of a family member, often all they see is a photo on the order of service. They would hear little about appearance from me, but rather the kind of person they were, their values, their faith in God (if any) and did they love and were they loved? Looks are only skin deep. Surely it's the message we give out that is more important than the looks of the messenger.

MEMORIES OF GAYBO

Gay Byrne

Being able to get RTE when I lived in Co Fermanagh, I became an admirer of Gay Byrne, who in his time was the most watched and listened to broadcaster in the Irish Republic. He was best known for his lifetime role as the anchor man on RTE's Late Late Show. For a record thirty-seven years on the show he had become one of the best known and respected broadcasters in the country. In 2010, the Irish Times said that Byrne was "unquestionably the most influential radio and television man in the history of the Irish State." In 2011, he was approached to become President of Ireland but declined to run, despite topping the opinion polls.

In the last few years of his life Gay took things a bit easier, but continued to host a Sunday evening programme called THE MEANING OF LIFE. On the programme he had a wide range of celebrities, politicians, actors, writers, poets and showbiz stars.

Gaybo, as he was affectionately known, asked questions about life. What's it all about? Why am I here? Is there a God? Why do bad things happen? What happens when we die?

He humbly suggested that like himself, few of his guests were religious experts, but all of them had at times had cause to think about the meaning of life. What is common to the series is Byrne's final question which always was, "If one day you die and you meet God (that's if you believe in God), what will you say to Him?" The answers he got from his guests are incredibly varied. Some said they had done their best. Many hoped at least to meet God's approval. Others were more cynical and would say things like "God, I've arrived." A few suggested that they couldn't envisage such a thing ever happening. One or two reflected on the wonder of being in the presence of God.

Knowing that I would never be famous enough to have been the guest of Gaybo, I would nevertheless be humbled and privileged to answer his final question, "When you die and meet God what will you say to Him?" My answer? "Lord, I have no right to be in Your presence. I am a repentant sinner who knows that Your Son Jesus Christ died on the cross to forgive my sins and to give me life in heaven. I have humbly claimed that promise and have had that assurance of salvation in my life here and look forward to the one to come. It is Your grace, Lord, and not my efforts that I am depending on." Gay Byrne died on the 4th November 2019. I often wonder how he would have answered the question?

LOCKED OUT

I had a friend, now deceased, who would often enjoy recalling a rather bizarre experience. Davy lived in a house in the Co Down hills which had an extension providing a shower. One morning as his wife left for work, thinking that Davy had also left, she proceeded to lock up the house without realising that her husband was in the shower room attached to the garage. When Davy realised what had happened he panicked, and realised that the only way out of the house was through the garage, but there he was without a stitch on. Never to be beaten, and rather resourceful, he looked around the garage, found some bin bags, and made himself a pair of trousers and a vest. Then he walked to a neighbour's house and rang the bell. Without even an explanation he asked her for the key of his home that she kept for emergencies. It's a bizarre and funny story and it always makes me laugh. I too have been locked out, but never quite as badly as in Davy's situation.

However, I am sure we have known what it's been like to be locked out of a relationship or not to be welcome in certain company. And as many of us know, being locked out in this community can easily happen. You might go to the wrong church, belong to the wrong club, or have a different political view, or your race, or your background make you different and unwelcome.

The late Peter Ward, a Redemptorist priest who served at Clonard monastery, once gave me a copy of a wonderful book he wrote with the title "The God of Welcomes." In it he recalled knocking a door in a north Dublin housing estate. After a time a young man came to the door, somewhat dishevelled and unkempt. Looking at Peter he exclaimed, "Oh Father, it's me mother yir lookin fir." "Why not you?" asked Peter. "I am no good," he replied, "I'm sponging on me mother." Peter's response was, "God loves you for nothin!"

Whoever may have excluded us or considered us unacceptable, and however much we live with hurts, God welcomes us. These well-known words of Revelation 3:20 come to mind: "Look! I stand at the door and knock. If you hear my voice and open the door, I will come in." It is never God who locks us out. If we may feel excluded by some of our family members, take heart, God welcomes us with the words of John's gospel, "To as many as receive Him (Jesus), to them gives He the right to be called the sons and daughters of God." - the best family of all.

Father Peter Ward

Clonard Monastery Belfast

WALKING IN THEIR SHOES

Salvation Army Music Corps

I have always had an affection for the Salvation Army. Lots about this Christian denomination appeals to me. When I was growing up I would look out of the window of my grandparents' home in North Belfast and listen to the band playing on the street. Many of their bands and songsters are outstanding. I have been honoured to be their guest preacher on several occasions and have always been inspired by their worship and music.

A friend who was training as a young Salvation Army officer in London told me my most memorable story of all. He was assigned to a congregation in London to work with a senior officer. One night they went out to bring some help to rough sleepers in London's cardboard city. One rough sleeper had made himself a pair of shoes. He had cut out some cardboard, inserted some twine and tied these makeshift shoes to his feet. The Salvation Army Officer in charge looked at him, and recognised his shoe size was close to his and stooping down he took his shoes and socks off and gave them to the man. He then took the cardboard shoes and  tied them to his own feet and proceed to walk back to the Salvation Army base in the cardboard flip-flops.

Walking in someone else's shoes, if they are the wrong fit, can be a very uncomfortable experience. (Hopefully some of the people who are homeless will get a pair of new shoes from the proceeds of this book.)

On the other hand, maybe I need to walk in the shoes of someone different to me.

I think of the dark days of the troubles in Northern Ireland. I often preach on the need to offer forgiveness to those who are the victims, and I am convinced how vital it is in releasing people from hurt. But I do understand their continual grieving when I sit in the home of a woman whose son was murdered, the reason, he was a community policeman.

I also recall many years ago a man contacting me about the horrendous murder of his daughter. He had travelled a distance and wanted me to take him to a certain spot, the waste ground where his daughter's murdered body had been dumped. She was a young woman taken from a nearly club and murdered. The reason for it? She was, according to reports, in the wrong place at the wrong time and was the wrong religion. I had two teenage daughters of my own. I stood with my arms around this fellow countryman and wept.

For a fleeting moment I was standing in his shoes and it did hurt.

NOT ABLE TO STAND FRANK SINATRA

STEREO

MY WAY FRANK SINATRA

ARRANGED AND CONDUCTED BY DON COSTA

MRS. ROBINSON
YESTERDAY
FOR ONCE IN MY LIFE
HALLELUJAH, I LOVE HER SO
WATCH WHAT HAPPENS
IF YOU GO AWAY
DIDN'T WE
ALL MY TOMORROWS
A DAY IN THE LIFE OF A FOOL
MY WAY

A friend of mine tells the story of preaching many years ago in a large Belfast church. In his sermon he related with great conviction the story of a man he knew well – a man called Tommy who earlier in his life had been a pub-club cabaret singer. Tommy had in the past many problems, indulgence in alcohol being one of them. But in later life he had a remarkable Christian conversion. He was always a Frank Sinatra admirer and sang all the famous Sinatra greats, including 'My way.'

Old Talk of the Town Cabaret Club Belfast

While sung by others, 'My Way' was supremely Sinatra's big hit. It spent seventy five weeks in the UK Top 40, a record which still stands. Sinatra was truly Tommy's hero and he sang this song with gusto in the popular night spots of Belfast.

After Tommy's conversion he kept singing, but found this song hard to sing, 'My Way' - surely not?" However, a local Christian songwriter rewrote the words and changed the familiar refrain to "I'll do it His way," meaning the way of Jesus, reflecting Tommy's commitment to walk the road of discipleship and make Jesus Christ the Lord of his life.

Shaking hands with the congregation at the conclusion of the service, my friend recognised a regular church-goer, a man who was an academic and lectured at the university. Knowing he wasn't given to praise, my friend was somewhat surprised when he warmly shook his hand and said with a rather plummy accent, "I really appreciated what you said this morning, Ken." My friend was encouraged but a little taken aback. He gently asked, "And what was it I

Roy Walker

said that you liked?" to which the man replied, "Well, I just can't stand Frank Sinatra!" I often laugh at the story, but then reflect on its seriousness. We might call it missing the point. My preacher friend only wanted people to hear the real story of what God had done in the life of Tommy who had been transformed by His grace. Sometimes we miss the point and don't hear what God is really saying to us. Perhaps it's because we really don't want to.

MAKE SURE TO CLAIM THAT VOUCHER

Dundalk destination

If you got gift vouchers for Christmas I hope you have spent them, or at least know where you've put them. I have had a few problems with them over the years. My recent one was last year when we left for a short hotel break. I left home at a leisurely pace and set off on the journey, but I soon came up with a jolt when my wife asked: "Have you got the voucher?" It was a moment of real embarrassment. I knew that without the voucher there was no admission to the hotel. So I realised my mistake and turned back, adding about forty miles to our overall journey.

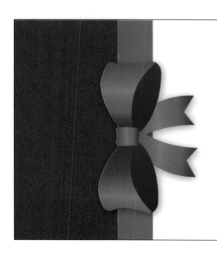

Gift
VOUCHER

God has pledged His love towards us.
Forgiveness, salvation from sin and the promise of eternal life
for evermore are waiting to be claimed.

IT IS FINISHED : PAID IN FULL

Later, my wife Carol in her own forgiving way smiled at me and remarked wryly, "Well, knowing you, you just might get one of your thoughts out of this!" The idea did come to mind. However, as I drove the car I considered my options. I wondered if the hotel would have taken my word for it, with the promise of the voucher in the post on our return. From experience I was taking no chances. My thrifty conscience reminded me of the millions of unclaimed vouchers that remain in the coffers of many hotels and major stores.

On our return my thoughts wandered in another direction. Significantly, Christians claim that the promises of God are vouched for and written in the words of the Old and New Testaments. They consistently tell us that God has pledged His love towards us. God promised a Saviour and He was born in Bethlehem. Fulfilling the many prophecies of the Old Testament, the message is that God is with us in Jesus Christ. The final words of Jesus on the cross - "It is finished" - mean

that the debt we owe is paid in full. Christ's birth, death and resurrection are crucial to the Christian faith and without them there is nothing to claim.

But there is something to claim! Forgiveness, salvation from sin and the promise of eternal life for evermore are waiting to be claimed.

I pray that having claimed God's greatest pledge of grace and forgiveness, imperfect as I am, I may share that love with whoever I meet, in whatever time God gives me in the days ahead. So don't forget to claim that voucher!

GOD'S SORTING OFFICE

It was one of those pre-Christmas days. The postman stuck a card under my door to say he couldn't deliver the item. So off I went in the rain to the sorting office. It was cold as we squeezed into a small room for shelter, with several more people outside in the rain. "Any more cards?" shouted a guy from behind the counter. As one man handed over his card, all that could be heard was the voice of an irate lady, "I was in front of you," she said loudly. The man looked, paused and then replied, "Oh, I am very sorry, I do apologise." The lady looked surprised but then said, "Oh that's okay." On that wet day in the melee of that small room it was hard to judge who was first in the queue. What impressed me was the gracious, gentle attitude of the man who gave way to the lady. I don't think it was what she had expected. It's certainly not always a characteristic of people in this community to give way. We are always very conscious of our rights. How often in life, relationships are damaged forever because one party will not give way and show grace. When confronted with a possible solution we often hear the comment, "You must be joking, no way!"

It made me think of how a willingness to give way and to say sorry can have an amazing effect on some of our relationships. But none more so than in our relationship with God. The lady in the sorting office said, "Oh that's ok," and I will never know her true feelings or how the man really felt about her response. Probably neither will ever remember this rather trivial incident.

Sometimes someone will say to me, "Reverend, I think he needs someone like yourself to sort him out." My response is to suggest that I can listen, and perhaps offer some helpful advice, but it will take someone greater than me to "sort him out", my thoughts being that if he is open to accept his failures before God, then nothing is impossible.

The Psalmist David, Israel's greatest king, made some mess of his life in his adulterous relationship with Bathsheba, along with his contriving and manipulation to cause her husband Uriah's death in battle. This he ultimately acknowledges with deep pain and repentance in Psalm 51. God sees the whole picture and knows everything about us. We have all sinned. However, if we accept our need for forgiveness, and are willing and honest to pray to God for a new start - be absolutely assured that this promise is true: "If we confess our sins to Him, He is faithful and just to forgive us our sins and to cleanse us from all wickedness." (1 John 1 v 9). When this happens we can experience the transforming power of God. Only He can truly sort us out.

Psalm 51 v 1 for personal meditation
*"Have mercy on me, O God, according to your unfailing love;
according to your great compassion blot out my transgressions.
Wash away all my iniquity and cleanse me from my sin.
For I know my transgressions, and my sin is always before me."*

Royal Mail sorting office Belfast

NOT THE WHOLE STORY

Once I wrote Thought for the Week for a newspaper but something happened; the last paragraph somehow got lost in transmission. When I picked up the paper on the Saturday morning what I read caused me some disquiet; it was not inaccurate, but unfortunately no longer told the whole story. While the article majored on the inability to put life's experiences into reverse, without the final paragraph it missed a vital truth about the One whose grace and forgiveness is the essential element in getting our lives together again, giving us a future that embraces forgiveness and hope.

However, that experience has had a positive outcome, leading me to this thought. It made me think of the number of times I have heard people express their concern that the whole story will never be told. Dealing with the past in Northern Ireland, I am conscious of the many victims whose hesitation with the idea of a Truth Commission is that "the whole story may never be told." Only recently I heard a victim of the Troubles say on a radio programme, "What's the point? We'll never hear the whole story." Often the saying is used to refer to those who are economical with the truth. This I hear quite often when I am offering support or help to a person, only to discover someone else bending my ear and cynically remarking, "Make sure you hear the whole story."

 I recall reading of a prisoner of war getting hold of a New Testament. Naturally he started at Matthew's Gospel. However, he gave up when reading about the torture of Jesus before His death, because coming from the violence of a prison camp he could take no more. A little later, returning to the story, he was transfixed by the resurrection story. This was for him news of hope.

If the last chapters of the gospels of Matthew, Mark, Luke and John had been lost in transmission, we might somehow have ended up honouring a hero who died for a

good cause, but little more. When Jesus appeared to the two disciples on the road to Emmaus as recorded in Luke chapter 24, he found them despairing, confused and distressed. The person they had followed had been crucified. It was all over! But when they recognised their companion was Jesus, "their hearts burned within them" and they returned to Jerusalem with great joy to share their experience of meeting the risen Lord. When we realise that Jesus Christ is alive and present with us, we too can experience the power of the One who forgives, restores and gives us hope forevermore. That is starting a journey that will enable us to discover the whole story.

Road to Emmaus

KEEP YOUR EARS OPEN WHEN ON THE TRAIN

"You're not listening," remarks my wife as she tries to get my attention. Some of us are talkers and I guess, if we are ministers, pastors or priests, we need to be good at it. Making conversation with people is a necessary skill, especially if people are "a bit reserved" as we say in these parts. But what about listening?

A friend of mine who was considered an expert counsellor always denied such a praiseworthy title; people would often say to him, "You really helped me," but he would quietly say to me, "I said very little, I just listened." I have often watched the famous Irish broadcaster, the late Gay Byrne; how he could lead a conversation and show such an interest in his guests that they opened up their lives and exposed their vulnerability.

I recall travelling on the train to Dublin one Saturday evening several years ago. It must have been bargain time in Belfast and everyone had been doing their shopping. The train was packed, when suddenly a few minutes before departure a number of women loaded with bags of shopping joined the train. I could smell their perfume the length and breadth of the carriage. The train was already packed and one could see some passengers getting a little tetchy by getting squeezed by the baggage and having to move over.

One young woman looked around to find a seat. She had no option but to sit beside me. I wasn't too sure if I welcomed her shopping bags crushing into me and disturbing my attempt to finish a book before we hit Connolly Station. I didn't show my slight irritation, I was polite and asked her about her bargains. She began to talk. She lived a few miles over the border from Newry. I asked her about her day in Belfast. The designer names on the bags suggested she wasn't short of a pound or two. Without much explanation about her day out, she diverted and began to tell me her story. She had troubles, hurts and difficulties in her life and several pressing issues. I tried to listen because I felt privileged. Suddenly she was getting off the train. I exclaimed, "You're away! I will pray for you. So nice to meet you." We were in Newry. I was disappointed. I would probably never see her again and I guess that suited her too. She had trusted me with her story. It's called intimacy with a stranger. Wherever and whenever she comes to mind I pray for her.

Words of the Book of James are worth reflection. "My dear brothers and sisters, take note of this: Everyone should be quick to listen, slow to speak and slow to become angry."

Train Station Belfast

Train Station Dublin

WHEN THE GUN WENT INTO THE RIVER

When I was ten years old we moved to the area of Belfast that joins Ballysillan to Ligoniel, known by the locals as the turn of the road. I recall the area to be a peaceful place where everyone got on well irrespective of their religion. My lasting impression was that the area was full of characters - one being Jimmy McCallum. A leader in Ligoniel Methodist Church, he was a great adviser and encourager to many. Sadly in later life he suffered from a stroke which caused him to be housebound. However, he continued his ministry from his front room, and his house became an open door for all sorts of people. One day he invited me to meet an old friend of his. "You need to hear his story," he remarked. "He always comes around on a Wednesday." The day came when I would meet this very old man, perhaps in his late 80s, in Jimmy's front room on the Ligoniel Road.

After some greetings and general chat, the old man told me his story:
"Son, in the 1920's there was trouble in Belfast and I got involved. I was given a pistol and told to go to a bar in the docks area. There I would seek out a man supposed to be in the IRA and at the appropriate moment I was to shoot him dead. On my way down the Newtownards Road I saw crowds of men cramming into the Methodist Church. Curiosity got the better of me and before I knew it, I was inside the church,

W.P. Nicholson

not knowing then that the preacher was the great evangelist W.P. Nicholson. At the end of the service he asked if any person wanted to surrender their life to Jesus Christ, then they should raise their hand and say, I will. Gripped by what I heard, I said, "I will." The service ended and I left, continuing on my way to the docks. As I crossed the bridge I stopped, took the pistol from my pocket and threw it into the River Lagan." With tears in his eyes he told me of the transformation that had taken place in his life since then.

What I didn't know then, was that around twelve years later I would become the minister of that same congregation on the Newtownards Road, now known as the East Belfast Mission. Looking back, I would have wished that many other men and women had thrown their guns into the Lagan, and found the transforming experience of knowing Christ that my friend had experienced.

Troubles on Belfast Street 1920s

Queens Bridge Belfast

NOTHING CAN SEPARATE

It was many years ago that I had my first conversation with Tom. Born on the Shankill Road in Belfast and in his early 20's got married. An entrepreneur, he did well in his job and soon gained promotion. "It was a collar and tie job," as he described it. But there was to be a secret shadowy side to his life. Encountering the troubles in Northern Ireland in the early 70s, he got involved with one of the loyalist paramilitary organisations. Although never directly involved in violence he was sympathetic to their cause and acted as an advisor. He would release statements on their behalf, and remained a business man to some, but to others was something entirely different. However, soon this contradictory life style would bring other pressures. He became a heavy drinker and this was accompanied by depression and despair.

Rev Tom

One evening in the 1980s as he left the Crescent Bar in South Belfast as he put it, surprisingly he ended up in the Crescent Church. Under the influence of drink he watched people emerging from the Tuesday meeting after listening to the well known Bible teacher Derick Bingham. Tom was somehow prompted by a voice within and sought help. The conversation that took place in the precincts of that Church with one or two of the leaders was ultimately to revolutionise his life. An eventual encounter with the living Christ would lead Tom on a new path. In 1989 he began to train for the Methodist ministry. In 1992 he became the minister of Belvoir Methodist Church in south Belfast. The 23rd September 1992 was to be a memorable but dreadful day. The nearby Forensic Science laboratory was destroyed by a terrorist bomb and the Church at Belvoir was left in rubble. On the morning following Tom was asked by a journalist, "well how's your Church Reverend? To which Tom, never short of an answer offered the profound comment "Oh my Church is alright it's the building that's the problem"

After a time of terminal illness Tom died in July 2007. How profound that statement was to become. The physical body Tom lived in was badly damaged and wrecked by illness, but the everlasting body he could claim was alright.

The words on those once admired loyalist murals containing the Latin phrase Quis Separrit "Who will separate." Had new meaning for Tom when, after his conversion, he persuaded his former friends to put the guns away and discover the forgiveness purpose and hope of a truly lasting relationship with God. As I watched him on the final journey it became more real than ever, his faith was as sure as the words of St Paul, "neither death nor life can separate us from the love of Christ."
'Quis Separrit' now has an eternal meaning.

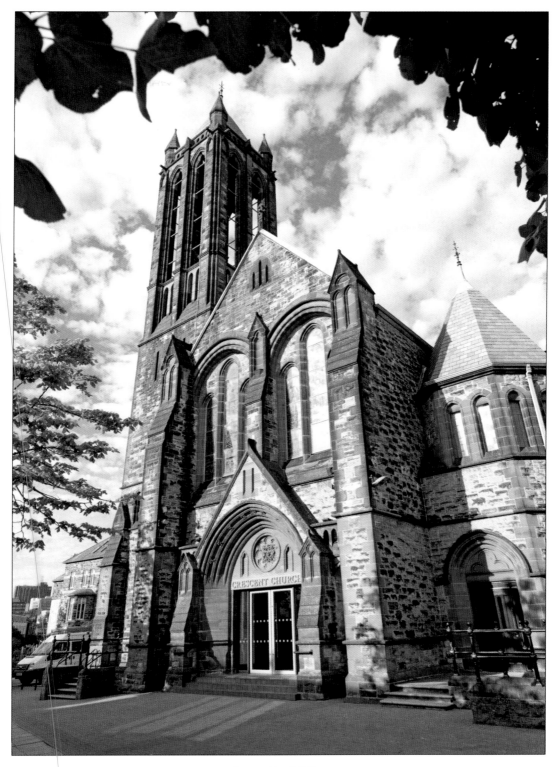

Crescent Church Belfast

TAKE A THIEF WITH YOU

One day I was challenged when I read about Major James Barker, who in 1883 led the way to establish the first Salvation Army social institution anywhere in the world on a permanent basis, known as the "Prison Gate Programme." It was in Melbourne, Australia, where Barker saw that prisoners being released from the Melbourne jails had nowhere to go and no possibility of work. So, sadly but inevitably, they re-offended and returned to jail. Barker leased a small house to provide accommodation for discharged prisoners. This led to the formation of the Prison-Gate Brigade, the members of which met discharged prisoners upon their release and offered them a home and the prospect of a job. Above all, Barker is known for his words to the prisoners telling them about the transforming power of Jesus Christ, and also for his most famous saying to his Salvation Army colleagues: "By all means aim to reach heaven, but be like Jesus and take a thief with you."

Reading this story I immediately recalled a personal story. A friend called Tom introduced me to Roy, a man who came from a chequered and disadvantaged background. He thought Roy would do well in our church fellowship as they were the kind of people who showed understanding and compassion to people irrespective of their backgrounds.

Roy had come to a Christian experience through a growing Belfast house church. My friend thought for some reason that I might also befriend him. As I got to know him, he told me a bit about his dysfunctional background. His father was an alcoholic and his mother died young. He was one of a large family. He recalled with regret that in his teens, he was a petty thief. He had spent several spells in young offenders' centres, known in my day as Borstals. One day I recall telling Tom that Roy was still a bit rough at the edges. A rough diamond! To which he remarked, "You have no idea what he was." I took his counsel and felt there was something about Roy that should cause me to persevere. He came to church every Sunday and to our prayer meeting, where he participated.

At least one person in the church chose to remind me for whatever reason that Roy was once a petty thief. I guess his remark was meant, as we say in these parts, to

"mark my card." I realised that Roy had literacy problems and hadn't a good formal education due to his waywardness. Nevertheless, he wasn't lazy and worked every day at his trade.

One day in the early 1980s, we met with Elizabeth, a teacher by profession. She suggested that she would help him with the basics of reading and writing. Knowing something about his background, she assured him that he wasn't a lost cause. She had great patience and my friend grew to trust and admire her. This eventually led him into Queen's University, where he

Major James Barker

Millisle Borstal

studied for a diploma. He then got the opportunity to work overseas with a Non-Governmental Organisation. Returning home after a few years, he went back to his trade and studied part time, and gained a Masters Degree from an English university. His life has not been problem-free and he is dogged with ill health. We often see each other and discuss theology and the issues of the day. My friend continues with his study of the Bible and reads widely. He is never shy of speaking to people about his Christian faith, and he always looks out for the poor and the underprivileged.

In moments of reflection, I remember Elizabeth sitting at a small table in that east Belfast home with Roy. Now gone home to heaven, she too, like Major James Barker, will have brought a thief with her.

Salvation Army Hostel

49

PRAYER AND WORK

I still recall hearing many years ago a rather funny story told on Radio 4 as a Thought for the Day. I am not sure of it's truth as it sounds slightly fictitious. The presenter told the story of a lady with her family taking an afternoon trip on a small fishing boat off the coast of Scotland. On board were two senior clergymen from the Church of Scotland. One was called the Rev Dr McHuge and large he was. The other was the Rev Dr Little and he was what his name suggests, tiny. Soon the little boat got into a storm and began to worryingly get tossed about. The lady with her family looked at the boatman anxiously and exclaimed, 'Boatman, do you not think we should ask these two good men of God to pray?' The boatman wryly smiled at the woman and then in a broad Scottish accent replied, 'Mam, why din ye ask Dr Little ta pray and hand Dr McHuge an oar.'

Sometimes when I have heard people pray, I know full well that if they did something about the situation their prayer could be answered. We might well pray for an end to a famine or a disaster at the other end of the world but if we are able to give financially and don't respond, what has been the value of the prayer? Perhaps we've prayed for peace in our community but in reality we have made little effort to build a friendship with someone from a different religious or political background? I have heard people praying fervently for peace in a church. But if I suggested, "Let's go to west Belfast and shake hands with some of the people. I can hear them say, "Oh you're stretching this too far.

There are those of course who did break the mould and ventured into friendships that have been lasting. But perhaps some in fear of what others might say or how their efforts might be misconstrued and criticised have simply stuck with praying - a worthy option or perhaps an easier one, preferring Dr Little's oar to that of Dr McHuge. The challenge is if at all we can, lets get hold of both.

I'M A NURSE IN THE CITY HOSPITAL

I still remember that dark wet winter evening as I sat in a line of traffic on Belfast's Great Victoria Street. Suddenly I heard screams and a commotion. As I got out of my car to investigate I immediately realised what had happened. There he was, a big heavy man lying on the road. I listened to the comments; "He got hit by that car as he staggered off the pavement." "He's the worst for the wear," "Aye no wonder people get killed when they drink like that," came a less sympathetic voice"

The blood was gushing from what appeared to be a serious head wound. On the ground stooped beside him there knelt a young women, who seemed to know what she was doing. As I stood by I couldn't help but notice her deportment and style, alongside the whiff of her expensive perfume. She was wearing an evening dress with well appointed jewellery. As the blood from this wounded stranger spurted out unto her dress, I remarked quietly,

"You're getting your dress ruined," to which she replied "It doesn't matter I am a nurse in the City Hospital."

I never knew the ultimate outcome of that incident, nor did I ever meet that young woman again, but her action has remained etched in my memory. She never asked the class or the creed of the stranger she attended, nor did she show any concern for the planned evening ahead, or the lovely dress that was probably ruined. Compassion had overtaken her, and she responded with out any pre conditions.

In a community, which is bedevilled by judgemental attitudes and has been known to murder and maim because of political attachment, religious belief, colour of skin, gender or just that somebody is different. I had met an ordinary hero, who will have received no honour or acknowledgement, other than the fulfilment and joy of having a compassionate heart.

When I think of what motivated that young attractive well dressed women, I have often wondered was it just the nursing instinct and the demand of duty to lay aside everything else to care when called upon, or perhaps it was her common humanity. Yet something suggests that whether she knew it or not, made in the image and likeness of God, she offered a glimpse of the nature of the One who out of incredible compassion spilled His blood on a cross, that some how we might discover the truth of the words of the New Testament writer John. "We love because He first loved us."

BURNLEY FOREVER!

Haslingden Methodist Church

In 1987 I went to the North Lancashire town of Haslingden to conduct some special services in the local Methodist Church. It was there that I met Carl Sudworth. We immediately got on well, in Belfast parlance, "like a house on fire." He was a cricket umpire, a leader in the Methodist Church and worked as sales rep for a confectionery business. Each time we met he had a chocolate bar to hand. He was also a committed supporter of Burnley Football Club. On the Saturday following my arrival he insisted that I be his guest at Turf Moor. I was thrilled by the possibility, for I had memories of the great Jimmy McIlroy who played for Burnley and was one of the great Northern Ireland stars of all time. When we arrived at the ground, I was treated with a visit to the Boardroom and presented with a Burnley tie which I cherish to this day. However I was disappointed to see only about 3000 people present in this large stadium, it looked empty. Burnley languished in the lower regions of the then 4th Division of the Football League. This once great club at the end of the 1987 season just survived, staying in the Football League on the result of their last game, and the day I saw them they were awful.

On the way home in the car Carl waxed eloquently on the demise of this great club. Yet there was one thing very obvious: nothing would shift his loyalty and support for the team. For him it was "Burnley forever" as he would exclaim come what may, rain, hail or shine, Carl Sudworth would be at Turf Moor.

Carl Sudworth with fellow supporters

You will understand my delight and his, when Burnley made it back into the Premier League. Perseverance, effort, talent, good management, support of their followers has played a part in their long return to top grade football.

I am always amazed at the commitment of many football supporters, their loyalty and perseverance. It is a lesson for those of us who declare ourselves as Christians. We too need to recognise that what happens to football clubs, in different ways happens to us. We struggle at times, we face criticism, doubts and tests. For some it can end in a lapse of faith, while others find faith strengthened and the experience enriching. Some pray and get though difficult situations and are amazed at the outcome. But such results don't always come instantly or perhaps at all and there is suffering, loss and disappointment.

My friend Carl Sudworth has suffered for many years from serious health problems. What is very obvious is that while he has that great loyalty to Burnley Football Club, his experience of life with its ups and downs has brought him to the point he will not just say, "Burnley forever," but as he once said to me "Jesus Christ whatever!" This is the Christian's hope knowing that whatever happens to us in the words of the Methodist founder John Wesley, "Best of all God is with us."

Jimmy McIlroy Burnley

ANOTHER KIND OF MIRROR

My abiding memory of January 1st is what happened to me a few years ago. I was still in bed at 10am after a late night to bring in the New Year. My get up early resolution was in the gutter. Wake up, I thought, as I hit the switch on the bedside radio. It was a phone-in all about New Year resolutions. "I want to try and stop drinking," comes the voice of one caller. Then the smokes get an airing. "I have tried to give up cigarettes many times, but I can't," says a concerned listener.

New Years Eve Belfast

Fielding the questions is a woman psychiatrist. "I am not sure whether I have an alcohol problem or not," says another caller, who claims to be very fit and able to jog three times a week, but confesses he drinks a bit, just maybe too much. I don't get the name of this psychiatrist, but now I'm listening, for this lady is good. As the programme is ending there comes her final unforgettable one liner, "Everyone needs to look at themselves in a mirror." Oh, I thought, I am about to do that and I don't look a pretty sight.

The man in the mirror

However, as I listened the memories flow back to the support meetings I have attended for recovering alcoholics, like Starous and some open meetings of Alcoholics Anonymous. Listening to men and women living in denial for their addiction they would blame a spouse, a difficult upbringing or a plethora or reasons as to why they were addicts, but then admit that it was really only when they looked at themselves. Sometimes they would quote steps 4 and 5 of the A.A. Programme.

Step 4: Made a searching and fearless moral inventory of ourselves
Step 5: Admitted to God, to ourselves, and to another human being the exact nature of our wrongs.

But then I reflect. What about me? I'm not an alcoholic, but I am still anything but perfect, only too aware of my own vulnerabilities and imperfections. I hope I have never forgotten the psychiatrist's, one liner as I look into my own interior mirror.

I am reminded that the Christian life isn't just a one off experience, rather an ongoing appreciation of the amazing grace of God in Jesus Christ that can enter my life everyday to help me overcome my failure and make me a better person. I still remain a work in progress. I can't do it myself.

As the programme ended with the expert voice of the psychiatrist I went to the bathroom to get myself pulled together only to observe the ageing process the outward appearance that I can't change much. Then I remember those familiar words from the Bible about how we humans look at the outward appearance, but forget that God looks on the heart.

BIRD MAN AND DINNER LADY

Billy at East Belfast Day Centre

Billy never said very much to me when I saw him having his lunch at the East Belfast Mission Day Centre. What was clear was, that he wasn't in the best of shape and not terribly mobile. What I did not realise at first was that he travelled a distance every day to our Day Centre to have his lunch. Tary McAfee our Catering Manager took a shine to old Billy and

Helping out at the Mission

really fussed over him. Billy always appeared to struggle with the basic things of life as he was quite physically disabled. But for the most part people didn't take much notice of him.

One day as I was moving around talking to the customers, Billy summoned me over to his table. "I have a problem," he said. He went on to explain that he kept birds (fair feathered kind) in his wee house on the Shankill Road. He explained that he had been to Ayr on a day trip and had purchased two little birds at a fair. Then with a forlorn expression he went on to say that when coming off the Cairnryan Ferry he had been stopped by an officer of the law who sternly asked where he was going with the two birds in the cage. "Home," he replied "I have lots of birds." The officer firmly told him he was going nowhere with the birds and if he tried, he too would end up in quarantine. His wee birds needed isolated for at least three months. Billy was distraught, but told me there was a way out. If I or someone who had no birds could look after them - even if they could stay with me in the leafy suburbs of east Belfast, all would be well. Billy

thought it would be far more comfortable for all concerned, including the birds. I wasn't sure, but after much bending of my wife's ear she agreed to allow the birds "bed and breakfast". Billy said he would supply the food, and I agreed to take them in. Billy knew more about feeding birds than I did, so I took his advice.

I went to the Larne ferry and collected the birds at the quarantine centre, signed the appropriate forms and brought them home. My wife insisted that if I was bringing in birds they should go to the attic. Every morning I would hear them chirping and would go up to see if they were in good shape. Then one morning there was no chirping. I feared the worst. As I entered the room I saw the two little birds lying dead at the bottom of the cage.

I was devastated, what was I going to tell Billy? I phoned my friend Tommy who was a bird expert. He told me the problem, they were on the wrong diet. He used the word "malnutrition" and I nodded in agreement. They needed some meat in their diet according to this expert breeder.

Now I had to tell Billy. On the way to his house I went to a local pet shop in Belfast, purchased two finches, put them in the cage and presented them to Billy. He was very gracious and understanding. As for my wife "no more birds in this house." As I often reflect on Billy's wee birds I recall the words of Jesus. "Are not two sparrows sold for a penny? Yet not one of them will fall to the ground apart from the will of your Father." If that was true of those wee birds how much more the Lord loved wee Billy even though he went through life largely unnoticed.

DAVY MY GRANDA

Jim with Grandad Davy

I grew up after World War 2 in the streets of north Belfast. My grandfather Davy McCaughrin was from Ballymena and came with his brothers to live on the Shankill Road in Belfast. This was for no other reason than to find work in the engineering industry. In my lifetime he worked in the Shipyard. He referred to himself as an iron dresser, often called a fettler, a person who grinds or sands down imperfections on metal castings. It was hard work, and in what was called "the hungry 30's "my granda was out of work for several years. I would hear what it was like to have no food. I was Davy's only grandson so I took pride of place in his life. I still recall this man hugging me as I met him coming off the tram from the Shipyard. He left the smell of the oil and dirt on my clothes. His needs were little and there wasn't a lot to spare. He and my grandmother lived in poor housing in Ottawa St. However they thought it was grand. Hard work meant he never sat in a church service on a Sunday morning but went on Sunday evenings to Agnes Street Presbyterian Church where I often a attended with him. He listened with great interest to what was then one of the Presbyterian Churches outstanding preachers, the Rev Donald Gillies.

Our Saturdays were taken up watching Cliftonville Football Club, the ground is called Solitude and in those days it was. Only a few hundred watched the Reds in those days and seldom did they win. My one regret is that grandad was gone when Cliftonville won the Irish Cup in their centenary year in 1979. In my days it was said that they were the strongest team in the Irish League (we held up the rest at the bottom of the league table,) unlike the successful Irish League Club of today.

I made lifelong friends at the Reds, one of whom was Jim Boyce who became Vice President of FIFA. A great ambassador for Northern Ireland. Another was Jim Greer with whom I went to school and played truant to watch Reds on a Wednesday afternoon cup replay with Glentoran seconds (only to be seen by our school teacher on the T.V. highlights that evening bringing a telling off the next day). Others included Liam Murray and the wonderful Christian ambassador Dessie Kirkwood. During those very the troubled years in north Belfast these men tried to address issues of sectarianism at the club and were shown respect for their efforts.

I often wondered about my grandfathers's outlook on life. He disliked the big house unionism of the day and supported the Northern Ireland Labour Party. Without a formal education he gave me oral history lessons on the Labour Party and how Keir Hardy came to parliament wearing a cloth cap. He told me I should value the National Health Service; it was hard won. My grandfather always resisted derogatory comments about Catholics. He didn't speak much about his faith. He went in a three piece suit on a Sunday evening to Church. The dressing up seemed to give him self esteem not found in the dirt and mire of the iron foundry. He would easily fill up with tears when he heard a gospel hymn. Five years before his death he confessed to me that he was a follower of Christ. On his death bed he recited to me the words of St John chapter 14.

I always really loved this man. He taught me moderation and respect towards others. Recently I made a discovery when I looked up the 1905 Irish census. A large family called McCaughrin lived in James St in Harryville they are all listed as Presbyterians all but one, my grandad's grandfather, my great great grandfather, was listed as a Roman Catholic. Had this something to do with who Davy McCaughrin really was? Someday I hope to get the answer.

Solitude - Cliftonville's ground

DESANOS

Desanos Ice Cream parlour on Newtownards Road Belfast

My friends know that I am very fond of ice cream. Living in east Belfast I find it hard to pass Archie Desano's Ice Cream shop on the Newtownards Road. This homemade Italian ice cream was hard to beat. I used to speak to the late Archie about his product and indeed about his interesting background. He told me how his father Pasquali had come from Italy to Belfast with the well known ice cream maker Fusco. However after a short time they went their separate ways and his dad set up his own ice cream stand.

He also became one of the first Italians to join the Orange Order so it's not surprising that he did a roaring trade around the Belfast Shipyard. I used to tease Archie indicating that if I had the recipe for his ice cream I would be millionaire. One day in for my usual treat, Archie handed me a tiny piece of paper with the recipe for the ice cream on it. "There it is you can have it but I tell you this, you'll never

make it." I did not have to be told that. Archie and a few of his family were the only ones that could make this product. It wasn't just the ingredients.They had learned the skills. The temperature needed in the process, the timing were all part of the making of this great ice cream.

I've never forgotten those remarks from the expert. "You can have the recipe but you'll never make it." It was Archie's hand that made the difference. It made me think of something much more profound.

While the early Christians as recorded in Acts c2 continued in the Apostles' Teaching, Fellowship, Breaking of Bread and Prayer, these were simply the ingredients. It was the intervention of a Divine hand, in the Person of the Holy Spirit who at Pentecost birthed the church and has at specific times in history caused that church to be revived and renewed.

Making it happen is much more than just a recipe.

SPEAK TO THE BACK OF THE ROOM

I never made much of my days at school, somehow I lost interest in my early education. The reasons would take too long to explain, but I do have at least one good memory. That was our music teacher Mrs Smyth. She took an interest in my playing of the clarinet in a local band. She seemed also to work on the principle of giving her pupils encouragement and wise words. Someone was doing their party piece when she spoke out loudly, "Speak to the back of the room. Speak in order to be heard." It was good advice. I never forgot her words and when I became a minister in the day when amplification equipment in the pulpit was often none existent or in it early developments I recalled her advice.

Reflecting on my old teachers remarks I have begun to see that they have an even more profound meaning. They represent in another sort of way those at the back of the room might I say on the fringe or just reading with a slight interest. That's why when I speak on the radio or as a guest at an event, I try to make sense of my faith with those with whom I stand on the terraces or the boundary. I want to be heard and might I add understood at the back of the room.

So I avoid language that is theological and unfamiliar. For example regeneration, mortification or sanctification as they may not be understood or heard by the person at the back of the room on the fringe of religion or Church. These are important words to be learned and explained. Jesus Christ God's son died on the cross. There He represented you and me. Somehow this was the way God dealt with our sins. Jesus took the responsibility. His rising again meant that he overcame the awful scourge of death. That was God's way of saying, this can happen to you and me.

We can live for evermore. We acknowledge our sinfulness; turn to Christ, and experience forgiveness and power of the Holy Spirit to live through this life. Then my hope is that we will have made life's greatest discovery. All that Jesus has achieved becomes ours. I hope this make sense to you if you think you are on the fringe at the back of the room. My hope is that it has been understood, heard and believed.

HE GAVE ME HIS GRAND-DAUGHTER

Alex Leckey (centre)

Robert Leckey was his name but I never knew him. Every year when the time comes around and I watch thousands gathering at cenotaphs in silent emotion, I remember Robert. He was a Gilford man and a Sergeant in the Irish Rifles. He was killed at the Battle of the Somme. He left behind a wife and nine children who were to experience a future of hardship and poverty. In the 1960s, while attending Shankill Methodist Church, I met his son Alex. Despite his tough early years and the little knowledge he had of his father, he had done well for himself, had served in the RAF and was a skilled tradesman. He and his wife Isabel had one daughter, Carol. In 1970 she became my wife. Some years later we visited the Somme war graves, but were unsuccessful at that point in finding her grandfather's grave.

The peace and tranquillity of those war cemeteries had a lasting effect on me. It was emotional! What was this all about, I thought, and was it necessary? What struck me forcibly was that the woman standing beside me, and our own three children, would never have been born had this man not lived.

What I would note on some of the gravestones was the common use of a text of scripture quoting Jesus Christ: "Greater love has no man than this, than he lay down his life for his friends." On the 1st July 1916 Robert Leckey certainly did that. What remains are his medals and a scroll acknowledging his sacrifice.

In contrast, St Paul maintained that Jesus didn't just die for friends. In fact, he died for enemies and sinners - a thought far beyond human comprehension. Not on the radar of many of us, quite unthinkable after the years of our conflict and pain.

But the greatest hope of all was when Jesus said, "Because I live you will live also." This

Jim and Carol

Christian claim is that by His death on the cross and His rising again, all who put their hope and trust in Him, from whatever age or generation, for them the sting of death is defeated and the confident hope of eternal life is a reality.

I am ever thankful to Robert Leckey who gave me his granddaughter, our children and grandchildren. But greater far is the hope given to us by Jesus Christ, whose gravestone will never be found, but who reigns in heaven for all eternity. Jesus lived, but more importantly, He lives!

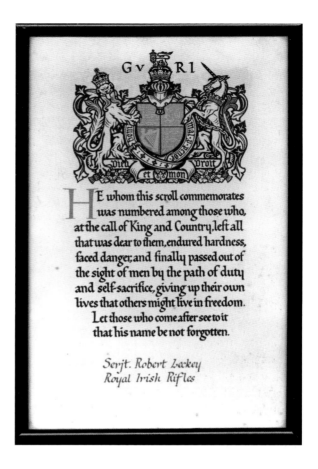

Gv R1

HE whom this scroll commemorates was numbered among those who, at the call of King and Country, left all that was dear to them, endured hardness, faced danger, and finally passed out of the sight of men by the path of duty and self-sacrifice, giving up their own lives that others might live in freedom.
Let those who come after see to it that his name be not forgotten.

Serjt. Robert Leckey
Royal Irish Rifles

Robert Leckey

WOOLIES

When I was a wee boy my father brought me most Saturday mornings to Woolworths or 'Woolies' in High Street, Belfast. It was the highlight of my week as we pushed through the crush (it was some crush!) and purchased some small item from the shop with my pocket money. Some years ago when I was visiting Pennsylvania, a local minister told me I was privileged to be in the town of Lancaster where Woolworths began trading, pointing out the actual shop as we walked by. On that winter day with icicles falling off my nose I didn't take time to stop.

F.W. Woolworth

F. W. Woolworth was born in 1852 on the family's meagre potato farm near New York. Not wanting to farm, he aspired to own a business. At 23 he started working in a store in New York. For the first three months he received no wage, because the owner's view was, "why should I pay you for teaching you the business?" While working there he observed that there would always be a table with bargain items priced at five cents. Woolworth liked the idea, so he borrowed $300 to open a store where all items were priced at five cents. He decided to open his first store near New York, but it failed within weeks. However a second store, established in Lancaster, Pennsylvania, was a real success.

Many local businessmen resented him and criticised his efforts.He eventually amassed a business empire and became a multi-millionaire with stores worldwide. His empire was passed on to others when he died at the age of 69 in 1919.

In November 2008 the UK Woolworths went into administration. Many thousands lost their jobs and the contents of the stores were sold to the public at unbelievable knockdown prices, bringing an end to a multinational company whose shops many of us loved to browse around.

I now feel a sense of sadness when I look down High Street and North Street in Belfast, where what was called the wee Woolworths traded. When I think of the demise of the firm, and indeed many of the great companies which have experienced global recession, I remain thankful for the enjoyment, the employment and the business they generated. A girl I knew worked in the High Street store, so as a youth, I would go in to see her and buy nothing. Not sure now of my motive!

Of course nothing stays static. History informs us that the best of enterprises go under. I can't help but recall the words of Jesus: "Do not store up for yourselves treasures on earth, where moth and rust destroy, and where thieves break in and steal. But store up for yourselves treasures in heaven, where moth and rust do not destroy, and where thieves do not break in and steal....... But seek first his kingdom and his righteousness, and all these things will be given to you as well." Matthew 6 v 19-21 & 33

Woolworths store Belfast

LABELS

Many years ago I attended a cross-community conference, with a well-known and rather outspoken women from east Belfast called Molly; she was feisty and would say it as it was, if she didn't agree with you. I once witnessed her confronting a group of what some of us call "hard men" who were about to paint offensive graffiti on a wall. Strong words were exchanged while I slipped away sheepishly. As we arrived at the hotel on the day of the conference Molly was offered her identity badge, with her name and the organisation she was representing. Adamantly she refused to accept, with the terse remark in her broad east Belfast accent. "You're not labelling me!" I had to laugh at Molly's stubbornness.

Molly Taylor

In a different kind of way it made me think about labels, and the way we very quickly stick them on people particularly in this community. Demeaning people by what we call them, I suggest contradicts the words, "Sticks and stones may break my bones but names will never hurt me." Words can cause great hurt.

Not unrelated, the early followers of Jesus were known by various names and some were not always that complimentary. It was in the 1st century in the city of Antioch that they got the label "Christians." Interestingly, this name would only

Newtownards Road Belfast

be used on two further occasions in the New Testament. Were the disciples proud to own the name? I guess they were because Christian literally means "Christ's one." So how could they not want to own that name.

The labels shown by our political allegiances, the behaviour of our communities and even the Churches we represent, may leave us ashamed at times. Many of us calling ourselves Christian have had to address our prejudice and sheer bigotry towards those who are not our kind. St Paul was certainly ashamed of his past outrageous behaviour, his bigotry toward the early followers of Jesus, but

Stewarts Supermarket Newtownards Road

eventually he would say, "I am not ashamed of the gospel, because it is the power of God that brings salvation to everyone who believes." Romans 1:16.

I often wonder how people label me? Some descriptions I may well dislike! For whatever reason, my friend Molly didn't want to be labelled, and I am not sure I want to be either. But if I am described as a "Christian," I am gratified to own that name, and to wear that label.

HALLELUJAH TO HANDEL

Dr Leslie Weatherhead

I like the rather amusing story told about the famous English preacher, Dr Leslie Weatherhead, who annually attended the Messiah at the Royal Albert Hall in London accompanied by his quaint and quite eccentric father-in-law. During the singing of the Hallelujah chorus, Leslie's father-in-law would stand up in the gallery and conduct the choir, much to his son-in-law's embarrassment! Each time the choir reached the words in the grand conclusion "He shall reign," the old man would push Leslie on the shoulder and say "How long, Leslie?" Then would come the loud choral response "for ever and ever." As the last notes of that grand chorus rang out the old man would turn to Leslie Weatherhead and say "Hi, Leslie, that is our Jesus they are singing about!"

It was indeed Jesus, they were singing about, and it is important that we don't forget that through the advent festivities and when we hear Handel's Messiah being sung we do indeed sing about Him. Yet how much better it will be when we see Him as He is and acknowledge Him with praise, honour, glory and power as the composer puts it "forever and ever." The music of composers such as Handel can bring spiritual

ecstasy in the immediate present. How much greater will our ecstasy be when one day we join that great choir, made up of multitudes no one can number and give praise to Jesus forever and ever. The question remains how do we get to this great event? Leslie and his father in law probably needed a ticket for the Royal Albert Hall. For that great future event the only ticket needed is a personal trust in Jesus as our Saviour and our Lord and a genuine acceptance of His grace and forgiveness. Then we will forever be able to shout "hallelujah".

Royal Albert Hall

A SAD END TO OLD GRUDGES

I couldn't help but notice Robert. He was one of those men who was always dressed immaculately. Getting to know where he lived I decided to give him a visit. It was then I realised that his first wife had died and he had remarried. Soon we became firm friends and being the kind of man who wanted to show generosity to his minister and realising we had a common interest in football, he produced two tickets for every home international that Northern Ireland played in the 1980s when they qualified for two World Cup finals.

I was soon learning more about my friend. After being widowed Robert remarried. However his only son John hadn't got on too well with Robert's new wife Mary and they all had become estranged. The issue had run very deep. Neither Robert nor Mary wanted to know about John. Like any minister I asked my predecessor about the situation. He seemed to know the whole story about John. He told me he was deeply saddened by the situation and that John now lived in England and that he had an occasional phone conversation with him. The whole thing seemed very petty.

Time marched on and Robert and Mary were living in an area of Belfast that was being redeveloped. They were given the choice of a move to the County Down coast to more suitable housing an opportunity not to be missed, and to be always away from the bricked up housing all around them.

Living by the sea was a great move, but sadly after a few years, Mary became unwell and died of a terminal illness. Talking to Robert I suggested he might consider reconnecting with his son, but he was having nothing to do with the idea. Some time elapsed and then Robert became ill and would spend several weeks in hospital. One day a consultant told him his condition was terminal. When I got to him, he was in tears. Again, I broached the subject of John "no, no, " he insisted, but his tone was a bit softer. On the next visit I tried again and his reply "not at the moment just leave it."

A few days later more quickly than I had expected he died. Several members of our church attended the funeral to pay their respects to this popular and generous man.

A few months passed-by when one day I received a phone call and when the caller gave me his name I gasped, he was Robert's son. He said "I have had a bad day. "I came over to Belfast and decided to look for my father. I went to the old house. The

conductor was wearing a white hat very similar to the one he favoured, he asked the conductor where he obtained it from.

"Man, haven't you heard of Mr Dickie Bird," he replied. "This is one of his hats. I took it off his head at the World Cup final... we all ran onto the field and I won the race."

Whether a person becomes famous or not isn't the most important thing. It is the word or deed that might turn a person's life around. You might never even know about it. Dickie Bird is famous, Alf Brodhead isn't but the both provide us with a profound truth.

The Book of Proverbs has a word for all of us:
Chapter 12:25 Anxious hearts are very heavy,
but a word of encouragement does wonders! NLT
Everyone enjoys a fitting reply; it is wonderful to
say the right thing at the right time! Chapter 15:23 NLT

Jim with Dickie Bird

THE ALL INCLUSIVE MURAL

Pope Francis

In the area where I grew up the paint jobs on the walls suggested that some people were not welcome, and this included a Church leader who lived in Rome. Indeed a man on a horse called King William was the hero and the only date worth remembering was 1690.

On two occasions the Roman Pontiff has put his foot in Ireland. I am sure if he made it across the duck pond to Norn Ireland or up from Dublin and got on a Belfast tour bus, he would soon get the message that in some parts it is still "No Pope here." He might also have a crisis of faith when he reads that God is in fact a prod. Now in fairness, the stuff on the walls has improved. The "murials" as they're better known are certainly better paint jobs than they used to be. Now they are seen as expressions of culture, and people with all kinds of accents stand around them clicking their cameras

Sandy Row Mural

Many will say we have come a long way in the last number of years, as reams of print roll out about our proposed shared future. Sometimes you might just get the impression that a future Pope could be asked to unveil the Orange arch in Sandy Row.

From my earliest day I began to question how people think in this community. Why should we want to exclude someone from a community because they are different to us? I would ask and would often raise an eyebrow from my elders. I had a desire for inclusiveness that valued each person. And I thought the Christian Church would be a good place to start, but later, becoming a minister, I would discover that sectarianism was never far away even amongst the most respected. Living in communities where territories are clearly marked out, the fear of the other is a breeding ground for suspicion and hatred.

One day watching highlights of a Gaelic match on TV, I noticed someone holding a banner. I recalled seeing it at a different sporting venue, Windsor Park the home of Linfield. John 3:16 it read. I didn't need to look it up. It was the cameo of Christian belief declaring "God so loved the world that He gave His only Son, that whosoever believes in Him will not perish but have everlasting life." That's God's mural I thought. So my prayer when

Gaelic football match

disagreement may still loom large, is that it won't just make it on to the walls, or onto banners, but into the hearts of Irish people that we will discover the God of grace who welcomes all.

Windsor Park Stadium

MORE TO LIFE THAN WEE RADIOS

Transistor Radio

Growing up in the 1950's in North Belfast I had an interesting school friend called Wilson. As soon as school was over I was out on the street kicking football, however Wilson would have none of it. He had another interest. In his little back room in his parents, two up two down

house on North Belfast's Ligoniel Road he built the earliest models of the transistor radio. He was totally addicted to this solitary lifestyle as he fanatically put these radios into plastic lunch boxes and sold them on to his mates at around three pounds a touch. It was a fortune in those days, but the radios worked well with the aid of a pair of headphones. So came my introduction to the B.B.C. Home Service and the Light Programme via the headphone. This young lad had achieved more than his footballing mates. Little did he know that he was "a pioneer," of what was to become the modern radio.

But there still is a twist to the story. Where we lived was close to the Horseshoe Road, as the locals called it where people would go walking. One day my mother called me over to the window of our little house and said with a glint in her eye, "Look out at Wilson, Jim!" There he was, my mate holding the hand of a very attractive young woman. My mother winked and remarked, "So much for the transistor radios today,"

That picture of the smiling Wilson with the attractive girl, who incidentally was to become his wife, has never left me. As I often reflect on this I can only think it was simply the joy of a new affection.

For some of us this new affection is much more profound; as it was for Saul of Tarsus a Pharisee, later known as St Paul, when he discovered of the transforming love of

Horseshoe Bend Ligoniel

God in Christ. He had been an opponent and persecutor of the Christian Church until he was dramatically converted to Jesus Christ on the Damascus road. He later wrote, "For me living is Christ and dying is gain."

THE HALLELUJAH MAN

Pastor Harry Toft

I recall a story told by a man who had an amazing impact on my early Christian life during the 1960's. He was Pastor Harry Toft, minister of the Ballysillan Elim Pentecostal Church. He would often tell the story of the man who couldn't be stopped from shouting "hallelujah." It must have been a rather non Pentecostal type of Church as they did not like this brother's outbursts. It was suggested that the minister should have a word with him. One Sunday evening he was called to the vestry, but as often happens the minister was to be distracted by another crisis. Leaving the vestry, he apologised to the man, telling him he would soon return and offered him a magazine to read. As he left, he chuckled at what he had given him, the National Geographical Magazine. "Not much there to shout hallelujah about," he thought to himself, but on his return he could not believe it, all he could hear from the vestry was this character resounding with loud "hallelujahs". What is this all about he wondered? Why are you shouting "hallelujah", he inquired? "Why", said the man, "have you read it? It says in this magazine that the Indian Ocean is at one point seven miles in depth and it says in the Bible in Micah 7 verse 19 "You will cast all our sins into the depths of the sea." That's why I'm shouting hallelujah."

Pastor Harry would then explain that no matter how sinful or terrible we have been, if we repent and ask God's forgiveness like the noisy man, we too can shout "hallelujah". I have often told that story and found it has brought encouragement to many people. The experience of so many to overcome past misdeeds, the haunting conscience, the nights of pain when people have wanted to put the clock back and change the past. The thought that God has buried our sins in the depth of the sea and that through Jesus Christ we can find full and complete forgiveness can be life transforming.

Unlike our human limitations to forgive; when God forgives he forgets. Worth even a muted "hallelujah." I am sure this story having being passed on through the generations has not lost anything in the telling but it makes a profound point.

NATIONALGEOGRAPHIC.COM/MAGAZINE APRIL 2007

NATIONAL
GEOGRAPHIC

SPECIAL REPORT

Saving the
Sea's Bounty

The Majestic Bluefin
Safe Haven in New Zealand
Village of Empty Nets

Hip-Hop Planet 100   Tallgrass Prairie 120   Leopard Lessons 142

THE SIN OF REMAINING SILENT

I will always remember Fred Craddock, who died in 2015. He was a famous American preacher who lectured on the subject at Emory University. I had the pleasure of listening to him in the 1990s at a conference in England. This introduced me to his writings, and particularly his amazing ability to communicate the gospel through personal stories.

One of the stories I remember is particularly relevant and poignant at this present time when racism is so much in the news.

Fred Craddock

Craddock tells that when he was a student for the ministry, around 11.30pm after studying all day he would go to a café. The owner got to know him and would gladly refill his coffee. The young Craddock would sit observing those around him as he contemplated his looming examination. One evening he noticed an old grey-haired black man coming into the café. No one came to serve him, until the man behind the counter shouted, "What do you want?" The cook then took a small burger, put it on a piece of bread and handed it to him. The usual condiments and napkin were not offered. The man went out the side door with his sandwich and sat eating it on the kerbside beside the garbage can. Craddock was deeply troubled by what he witnessed.

Emory University students USA

I have never had such an experience myself of witnessing a black person being demeaned like that. If I did I hope I would protest loudly. But sadly in this country it does happen more often than we want to admit.

However, to my shame I have listened to sectarian comments regarding a person's religion and gender, and have heard the well-off speak of "those who will neither work nor want", and "those foreigners coming into our country to take our jobs". I can't say that on every occasion I have spoken out. I want to be well thought of, too much perhaps. I may want to avoid a row and have remained silent.

Fred Craddock concludes his story: "I didn't say anything. I did not reprimand, protest, or witness to the cook. I did not go out and sit beside the man on the kerbside. I didn't do anything. I was thinking about the questions coming up in the exams. As I left the place and went up the hill to my room to resume my studies, off in the distance I heard the crow cock."

In his own subtle way, Fred Craddock is referring to Peter's denial of Jesus. It is a reminder to us that there are more ways than one to deny Christ.

REFEREE

"Referee!" I had often heard this word shouted in anger at Solitude, the home of Cliftonville Football Club, where I spent the early years of my life following the Reds. My grandfather would often give his verdict on the performance of the referee. Sometimes it was very unfavourable! However, one referee in particular, Malcolm Wright, seemed to have his approval as he had great authority over the players and seldom let the game get out of control.

In 1999 when I became the minister of Thomas Street Methodist Church in Portadown, I would occasionally notice a face in the congregation, and somehow even after many years, I thought I recognised him. He was the famous Malcolm Wright, former Irish League and

Malcolm Wright

International Football referee. As I was his minister I had the privilege of being in his home on several occasions and we had much to talk about. I would reflect on the 1979 cup final at Windsor Park when I was thrilled that Cliftonville, in their centenary year, beat Portadown 3.2 in the Irish Cup Final. It was a cliff-hanger of a game and Malcolm was the referee. "What do you need to be a referee?" I asked one day, to which he replied, "You need to be without fear and stick to your decisions."

England v Wales - Shilton in Goal

He explained that, however much he received abuse and threats from the sidelines, he never changed his mind.

I was to learn other things about him. In the 1964-65 season he was accepted by FIFA as an international referee, a position he held until 1979. During his lifetime, Malcolm refereed five Irish Cup finals - which is still a record to this day. Malcolm's travels as a referee took him far beyond the Irish League to clubs around Europe. One of his highlights was officiating at a World Cup qualifier between England and Wales at Wembley.

After retiring from the game, the IFA general secretary asked Malcolm to take on the task of re-organising the refereeing structure in Northern Ireland – a position he held from 1980 until 2004. Malcolm was famous in world football circles. But there was so much more – we shared another interest. Brought up in the Salvation Army, he was an accomplished cornet player and musician. He was the conductor of a number of bands, including Roughan and Thomas Street Silver Bands.

One wet, windy day when I was at a funeral my umbrella blew inside out. When I returned home my wife Carol said that Malcolm had called and left me a beautiful high-class umbrella. That was typical, and many years later I still treasure this gift.

Of all the memories I have of Malcolm, one overshadows the rest. One Palm Sunday, after a service, Malcolm drew me aside and told me that he had committed his life to Christ and had an assurance for the first time of God's grace and acceptance. I still recall the night when he told his story of his Christian assurance in Epworth Methodist Church, Portadown.

After I moved to work in north and west Belfast in 2006, Malcolm's musical prowess brought him back in his final days to the Salvation Army at Portadown.

On a June day in 2016 he heard the trumpet call of the ultimate referee, the Lord Himself. I look forward to meeting this humble, talented and generous man again in the life that never ends.

TRUE PROGRESS

I still recall the day when my grandfather purchased a combined Regentone Radio and record player. He thought it was an amazing invention and it worked from his recently installed electricity supply. He didn't possess a telephone - such a wonder was only found in a red kiosk or at the corner shop, to be used only in dire emergencies.

Regentone Radiogram

A shipyard man involved in building engines for Harland and Wolff's big ships, he was well clued into modern developments. He would often remark, "You can't stop progress." He was not a bit overawed when we all piled into our two up, two down house to watch the 1954 FA cup final, between West Bromwich Albion and Preston

1954 FA cup final

North End, albeit on an early black and white television that suffered from several intermittent problems. When the picture slipped as it often did, my nine year old nimble hands were called for to fiddle with the adjustment nob on the back of the TV.

An incident sometime ago made me reflect on all of this when I called to see a neighbour, "Say hello to David, he's waving at you," she remarked, as she stared into

her iPad and spoke to her son waving all the way from Dubai. We greeted each other warmly and shared a few words. It caused me to think of my grandfather and his comments about progress; I wondered if I had said to him, "Progress? That's nothing! I will have friends thousands of miles away talking to me in the same room, showing me their children and raising a cup of tea at the same time." I could have seen the old man lugging me down to the G.P. As we say in these parts, "to have my head examined." For him such a conversation would have sounded insane.

For many people belief in an afterlife is viewed with similar skepticism. Yet, if at a human level continents, can be crossed in seconds and people can appear on a screen in a flash, is it not believable that there is a life and a world of communication and real relationships beyond this one. St Paul tells Christians in Corinth that, What no eye has seen, what no ear has heard, and what no human mind has conceived, (are) things God has prepared for those who love him. 1 Corinthians ch 2 v 9. NIV

The Bible constantly affirms, that Jesus Christ goes to prepare a place for those who love Him, This makes the future bright and the world to come a better place better by far. No death, no pain, no separation, summed up in the words of St Paul when he writes, "For I consider that the sufferings of this present time are not worth comparing with the glory that is to be revealed to us."

In the days ahead, whatever happens, these great and positive assurances remain the sure and certain hope of every Christian believer.

AMAZING GRACE

Alf McCreary

It was the afternoon of 24th June 2020 when my phone rang. It was Alf McCreary, the well-known Belfast Telegraph journalist. He reminded me that on Saturday the 27th it would be the 25th anniversary of the death of Gordon Wilson. He asked if it would be possible for me to offer a few words about Gordon, as he was doing a feature for Saturday's edition. I knew of Alf's link with the Wilson family; in 1990 he had co-authored an amazing book with Gordon entitled 'Marie'.

As I reflected on Alf's request, my mind went back to meeting Gordon Wilson for the first time in 1972 when I became a minister in Irvinestown in County Fermanagh. He was a well respected Enniskillen businessman who took over the large drapery shop from his father. Gordon was originally from Manorhamilton in County Leitrim in the Irish Republic.

Seeing him outside, I would notice how tall he was. He was always recognisable by the large strides he took. Mostly I would meet him in church circles in Fermanagh. "How are you, young fellow?" he would greet me. This would always be followed by a bit of humorous banter.

Gordon Wilson

Remembrance Day bomb attack Enniskillen

In 1978 we moved to work on the Newtownards Road in east Belfast. In October 1986 I was invited back to Enniskillen to Darling Street Methodist Church to take an evening Harvest Service. After the service a young woman, full of smiles, approached me and asked if I could give her a lift to the Royal Victoria Hospital where she was a nurse. I couldn't oblige, as I was staying in the area to take another harvest service on the Monday evening. It was Marie Wilson, Gordon's daughter, and I was never to see her again, for in November the following year she was killed in the Enniskillen bombing. I still regret not having that couple of hours with her on the journey back to Belfast that evening.

I was just about to leave church on Remembrance Sunday 8th November 1987 when I heard the breaking news from Enniskillen. In the early afternoon I received a phone call giving me more details. The voice trembled. "Gordon Wilson has been seriously injured, but we think Marie Wilson is dead." Feelings of shock, anger and hopelessness began to take over. Final news: twelve killed and sixty-three injured. The country was in shock and there was outrage.

The following morning on the radio I heard these words from Gordon Wilson:

"She held my hand tightly, and gripped me as hard as she could. She said, 'Daddy, I love you very much.' Those were her exact words to me, and those were the last words I ever heard her say."

Marie Wilson

Gordon and his wife Joan

To the astonishment of listeners, Wilson went on to add, "But I bear no ill will. I bear no grudge. Dirty sort of talk is not going to bring her back to life. She was a great wee lassie. She loved her profession. She was a pet. She's dead. She's in heaven and we shall meet again. I will pray for these men tonight and every night."

A few nights later, the badly injured Gordon attended a Catholic Mass in Enniskillen filled with people from both communities, where he was applauded into the church. I know that not everyone would have agreed with this gesture, nor his words on the media. Despite his grief and that of his wife Joan and the family, he took it all with grace. I thought of his large strides.

Gradually this quiet, unassuming man became a public figure and an active peacemaker. As I got to know him better, and now living in Belfast with people being murdered almost every day, I sought to engage him with the loyalist paramilitaries. In a conversation he told me of a clandestine meeting he had had with the Provisional IRA. Sadly, he was disappointed and felt it came to nothing. But I felt sure they couldn't meet Gordon Wilson without having been impacted by his amazing Christian aura.

Not long before his death, I took him to meet the leaders of the UVF on the Shankill Road. Whatever the prior information was, the venue was changed twice as it was thought that there might be a bomb attack on the building. Gordon remained unfazed. Eventually the meeting got under way, and I watched the three UVF men moved to tears as Gordon pleaded with them to give up their guns and move forward. It was obvious he was sowing seeds of hope when they admitted to him that the troubles had to end as there was no future in violence.

A few years later the IRA and the loyalist paramilitaries called a ceasefire leading to the peace process and what still remains a very fragile shared government in Northern Ireland. While things are not perfect they are much better.

As historian Jonathan Barton wrote in 1994, referring to Gordon Wilson's remarks on the day after the bomb, "No words in more than twenty-five years of violence in Northern Ireland had such a powerful, emotional impact."

Sadly, in December 1994 Gordon and Joan's son Peter was killed in a tragic road accident. Six months later on the 27th June 1995 Gordon died suddenly. Only the Lord who called him home will fully know about the part he played in bringing peace to Ireland, the place he loved so dearly. He was unapologetically an Irishman, and was honoured by the Irish government when he became a Senator. He took large strides for peace.

When I think of Joan and Gordon, two words come to mind, "Amazing Grace."

NO JOY ON THEIR FACES

It was in early 1972 that I met Willie McAran for the first time. A true character! His wife Lily was a member of the Trillick Methodist Church and they lived near Maralough Chapel on the County Tyrone/Fermanagh border. Willie smoked a pipe and was something of a homespun philosopher.

The house was something else. In the corner were two stacks of newspapers about three feet high, one the Impartial Reporter and the other the Tyrone Constitution. I often wondered had these newspapers transferred their archive centre to Willie's house.

These local weeklies provided Willie with a window on the world. My challenge was how to talk to Willie about the Christian faith, knowing he was a little sceptical. He generally agreed with much of what I was saying. He had no problem with Jesus, but wasn't sure about his followers. I was a Belfast man coming from the troubled streets of the city to the quietness of the countryside, where neighbours lived side by side whatever their religion. Willie was all for live and let live, a strong critic of extremists, and when they popped up as professing Christians Willie was on the front foot with his scepticism.

One day on a visit to Willie I knew something was smouldering in his mind. As he blew the smoke from his pipe he asked, "Reverend, would you say Christianity is a religion of joy?" "Yes of course it is," I replied. "Well, take a look at this," said Willie, and picked up the most recent copy of the Tyrone Constitution and pointed to a picture. It was a church opening where the photographer had taken a photo from the pulpit. Then says Willie, "Wouldn't you think they were sitting in front of a firing

squad?" Oh, they did look glum and I had to laugh, but it affirmed Willie's perception of some Christians.

I did understand his sentiments. Christianity is a serious commitment. It is not all laughter and levity, but it is joyful, even though there are times when people don't feel like smiling. However, a church opening is surely worthy of a smile.

My good friend Church of Ireland Bishop Ken Clarke once said to a congregation within my hearing, "If you have joy in your hearts please inform your face!" As far as Willie was concerned, if there was any joy it wasn't to be seen on the faces in the photograph.

The words of Proverbs and Philippians are worth noting:

"Rejoice in the Lord always.
I will say it again: Rejoice!"
Philippians 4:4 NIV

"A cheerful heart makes you healthy.
But a broken spirit dries you up."
Proverbs 17:22 NIV

Bishop Ken Clarke

THE REASON WHY

Queen's Elms

One beautiful Sunday evening in September 1983 I made my way to Queen's Elms, where Prison Fellowship were having their world conference in Belfast. My friend Robert Russell, one of the prison chaplains, informed me that if I went along I might get a few good interviews for Downtown Radio's Church Window. I was one of a team of five who produced the programme. I thought I might get a scoop as Chuck Colson was present, Richard Nixon's aide, who went to prison for his involvement in the Watergate scandal. Robert Russell mentioned one other person, Rita Nightingale. I had heard about this woman's story on the news, so I was pleased when she agreed to an interview. I was ushered into a small room and there she was, smiling, a radiant personality with a melodious Lancastrian accent. In the fifteen minute interview I got the gist of her story.

Life was wonderful for this beautiful young woman in one of Hong Kong's exotic nightclubs. A mistress of a rich and attractive Chinese playboy, she lived a life of excitement and glamour.

However, it all came to an end in this way. After some time she decided to make a visit home to England. She

Charles Colson and Richard Nixon

stopped off at Bangkok airport and was searched. To her horror, the man she had recently been with had hidden heroin in her baggage. Innocent though she was, she was nevertheless jailed for twenty years.

Rita paused for a moment, then she explained that after nine months in Lard Yao prison, she was told that a lady was stopping off in Bangkok and had arranged a prison visit to her on her way to see her daughter in Australia. Martha Livesey was from Blackburn and had read in the local press about a young woman from there being in prison in Bangkok. As she would be making a short stop over in Bangkok, she was able to arrange a visit to Rita.

"When I heard the Blackburn accent I burst into tears," Rita went on. "She was white-haired, frail and neatly dressed. 'I'm Martha Livesey,' she said, "I've come to see you, love, because I'm from Blackburn too.'"

It was hard to hear Martha through the noise in the prison, but she could read the sympathy on her face. Rita said that going back that day into that dirty cell she was hysterical. Martha had left a gift of fruit, but then she noticed that tucked inside it there was a Christian booklet called 'The Reason Why' I nodded to Rita as I was familiar with this booklet written by Robert Laidlaw, a New Zealand businessman. Then she explained that the message in the booklet overwhelmed her, it was the story of Jesus and the wonder of his forgiveness. Suddenly, Rita told me, she was overcome by the love of God and the transforming power of Christ.

However, this was not the end. A further period of prison faced her, but after a three-year campaign by the British government and many others, she was eventually freed and granted a pardon from the King of Thailand.

Rita now works in a Christian ministry with prisoners in Bulgaria. I will never forget that deeply moving night in Belfast when I interviewed her.

Nor will I forget about Martha Livesey or Robert Laidlaw, both used in a significant way to bring God's grace to a remarkable woman.

Rita's story can be read in her book 'Freed for Life.'

RANGERS PLAY BETTER ON THE RADIO

I have always admired radio football commentators it for me requires more skill than when commentating for television. One of my favourite commentators is Alan Green. a former pupil of Methodist College in Belfast. So it's always a joy to hear his Northern Irish accent on the Radio. He has amazing ability to use descriptive language, word pictures that capture the scene.

I recall Alan Green being asked towards the end of his Radio 5 days what was the secret of being a good radio commentator. Green remarked, "I commentate as if everyone is blind." I found his insight enlightening.

Alan Green

It also reminded me of a much more lighthearted story. In my days at the East Belfast Mission a Glaswegian called Mal lived for a short time in our newly built hostel. I soon realised that he was a dyed- in -the wool Glasgow Rangers supporter. On a Saturday afternoon he could just about manage to tune his little portable radio to Radio Scotland. Very often the commentary was from a Rangers match.

Having a lifelong interest in football, in the early 1990s I installed Sky Sports. On one occasion I noticed that on the TV schedule Rangers were playing their biggest rivals Celtic. Down at the Mission I saw Mal and called him aside and suggested that he be my guest the next Saturday to watch his team on TV. To my surprise, he bluntly refused. For a moment I thought perhaps Mal was slightly bashful and didn't want to come to our manse in the leafy suburbs of Cyprus Avenue. I became a little more persistent but Mal was not to be convinced. He looked at me with a smile and remarked. "Rangers play better on the radio." Humorous though it is, I understood.

It also made me think of some remarks made by the principal of Edgehill College, where I trained for the ministry. The late Rev Richard Greenwood in May 1970 addressed the students leaving college to make their way to their new appointments. "Don't forget the importance of the public reading of Scripture." While he advocated regular reading and study of the Bible he was adamant about the importance of having it heard.

Rev Richard Greenwood

It has taken me some years to understand the profundity of that statement. Nowadays, in some churches I often only hear snippets of scripture read. Recently in this lockdown and with my Bible to hand, I have begun to listen to the famous actor David Suchet read the scriptures. To hear them read so well, brings me into another world. Suchet is doing in a similar way what Alan Green was doing for his audience. As I listen I am translated into those scenes from the Bible even though I cannot see them with my eyes. Much better than listening to Rangers play better on the radio!

Verses from two of my favourite Sunday school hymns come to mind.

I sometimes think about the Cross,.
And shut my eyes and try to see,
The cruel nails and crown of thorns,
And Jesus crucified for me.

But even could I see Him die,
I could but see a little part,
Of that great love which like a fire,
Is always burning in my heart.

William Walsham How, 1823-97

Tell me the stories of Jesus
I love to hear;
Things I would ask him to tell me
If He were here;
Scenes by the wayside.
Tales of the sea,
Stories of Jesus, Tell them to me.

William H. Parker 1845-1929

St Paul writes; "Until I come, devote yourself to the public reading of Scripture, to preaching and to teaching." 1 Timothy 4:13 NIV

PROMPTINGS

Old Portadown

In 1999 my life took a surprising turn. Having worked in east Belfast for 21 years at the Methodist Church, which became the East Belfast Mission in 1985, it was decided by the Methodist Conference to station me in Thomas Street Methodist Church in Portadown with the oversight of seven congregations, with numbers on Sunday ranging from 10 to over 200, Thomas Street at the time being the largest.

Rev Dr Bill Davies

I did have great reservations about this, as I would have been happy to remain in east Belfast for some further years. However, in July 1999 we were to move to Portadown.

Something unusual happened in the weeks before we left, when the study in the manse required a new window. Interested in watching the window fitter remove the old window, I got into conversation. I told him that we wouldn't be around to enjoy the new doubled glazed window as we were moving to Portadown. At that point he began to carefully remove newspapers that were stuffed in the cavity around the window.

He remarked that these old newspapers were always interesting to look at. Suddenly he spread one out on my desk. It was a 1950 edition of the Belfast Newsletter.

Thomas Street Methodist Church Portadown

"Look!" he said in amazement, "there's where you are going." On the front page was a picture of High Street Portadown. I was taken aback - was this confirmation from God? I prayed it was.

Simply coincidence, some might say. The Rev Dr Bill Davies, a former President of the British Methodist Church, has been a mentor to me. In the 1970s Bill was deeply involved in the Renewal Movement on these islands; when he preaches there is a sense of the presence of God. When he was visiting Portadown to preach at Thomas Street, I showed him the picture. Looking at the old photo of Portadown he remarked, "No coincidence, that's the Holy Spirit." I often recall the words of the late Archbishop William Temple, "When I pray, coincidences happen, and when I don't, they don't."

PRODS

Newtownards Road

I remember as a wee boy going to the Falls Road to see friends with my mother. Being a stranger to the area a little girl looked at me on the street and asked if I was a Prod. I recall feeling slightly scared.

One evening in June 1999 a week before leaving Belfast for Portadown our neighbour Theresa Judge asked if I would come in to see her. The Judges were wonderful people with a very moderate political outlook. It was nothing unusual to call by to see Theresa, a woman in her 80s I knew there was something on her mind as she paused hesitantly to get to the point to inform me that Breandán Mac Cionnaith the leader of the Garvaghy Road residents was her nephew. "I think knowing you, you will probably meet him and I would want you to know."

A few weeks after arriving in Portadown I decided to meet Harold Gracey the Grand Master of the Portadown District Orange Lodge. Harold in protest had decamped to a caravan on grounds near Drumcree Church. Not sure how he would receive me, to my surprise, he was welcoming and pleased that I was showing an interest in what was going on. I informed him that on the following day I was hoping to meet Breandán Mac Cionnaith. To my astonishment Harold suggested that such a meeting could only do good. Kenneth Twyble, Unionist Councillor and former Mayor of the

Borough was a Methodist Local Preacher. He had always kept lines open with the residents, not always well received by the Orangemen or their supporters. He had many dealings with Breandán MacCionnaith and so arranged the meeting. This was the prod I needed.

Harold Gracey

Breandán was a former IRA prisoner. I perceived that for him some PRODs were a problem. On arrival he immediately welcomed me. "You know my Auntie Theresa and she thinks well of you." Suddenly all barriers came down. From then on I had several separate meetings with Breandán and the Orange leaders. After some time Ian Milne a Funeral Director and an Orangeman at the time agreed to meet Breandán MacCionnaith. Ian had a strong desire to see the Drumcree issue resolved as he had experienced traumatic personal loss as a former member of the R.U.C. We both agreed to meet

Breandán Mac Cionnaith

Breandán albeit secretly in the home of the parish priest. The meeting went well. This affirmed my view that both sides needed to talk. This led to numerous conversations and the involvement of the South African Human Rights Lawyer Brian Curran, who was involved in his country's Truth and Reconciliation Commission. Through time, many played a part including Ian in helping Portadown get back to normality. The local Portadown District no longer welcomed people and bands from all over Northern Ireland at Drumcree. Face to face talks over Drumcree to my knowledge and to date have not happened. However the tension and division is no longer apparent. I consider that I only played a small part in diffusing things, for that I was privileged.

Things sometimes need a "PROD."

MY LASTING MEMORY OF JOHN HUME

John Hume, Jim Rea and Deputy Mayor Mildred Garfield

I still recall the night I met John Hume in the city he referred to as Derry. I too call it Derry, not for any political reason, but more because of I associate it with watching Derry City in the Irish league in the 1960s.

In March 2004, as President of the Methodist Church I was invited by the Rev Sam McGuffin, then Superintendent of the Derry City Methodist Mission, to their anniversary weekend to open their Family Centre, and to dedicate the newly built Men's Hostel for the homeless in the city.

At the Sunday evening service I looked down into the congregation, only to see the famous politician John Hume sitting near the front of the church with his wife Pat. John was known to attend special events in churches of varying denominations. I knew a lot about John Hume, though he probably knew little about me. In my community, reactions to John Hume were somewhat mixed. Generally, working class unionists saw him as a strong promoter of a united Ireland. But I believe history will judge him generously, because he was primarily a peacemaker. His desire for a united Ireland was based on a unity of hearts and minds and not just territorial land unity. He urged his supporters to spill their sweat and not their blood, and reminded all of us that you can't eat a flag.

Most memorable will be the secret Hume/Adams talks in Clonard Monastery that ultimately led to the IRA ceasefire.

At the end of the service that evening, during the tea John Hume spoke warmly about the amazing contribution of the Methodist Mission to life in the city. Later I had an opportunity to talk with him. He was, as I expected, unpretentious and pleasant.

But the memory of that evening pales into insignificance beside my truly lasting memory, and perhaps what is less well known of Hume. He was co-awarded the Nobel Peace Prize in 1998, and added to the award was a sum of almost £300,000.

So what did he do with this money? He gave it away. There were several charities, but two of the biggest beneficiaries were St Vincent de Paul and the Salvation Army.

Pamela Neill, then public relations officer for the Salvation Army, said that John Hume's contribution to their work went beyond the monetary value. She was so happy to be able to tell people about how much Mr Hume had done to relieve poverty in Northern Ireland, reminding people that he could have kept the money. In her final remarks Pamela suggested that what John Hume had done was immeasurable and should be shouted from the rooftops.

With all my memories of John Hume's political career and that night in Derry/Londonderry, this act of generosity remains with me more than any other. Characteristically he never did shout it from the rooftops.

I am reminded of the words of Jesus,

"But when you give to the needy,
do not let your left hand know what your
right hand is doing."
Matthew 6:3

John Hume died on 3rd August 2020. He was a giant in Irish politics.

WHEN A TENNER IS AN ANSWER TO PRAYER

In life occasionally we have unforgettable and special moments. Because they are rare they remain etched in our memories. Being a cricket fan in the 1980s and 1990s, I was a regular attender at the annual Scarborough Cricket Festival in Yorkshire, a three-day tournament in which two invited English county teams play a knockout competition against Yorkshire and Lancashire. It was a great festival at which I met one of my heroes, the famous umpire Dickie Bird. I considered this to be my special moment of the visit. But it wasn't!

Scarborough Cricket Festival

Scarborough Cricket Festival

In those days I was a motorcycle enthusiast, not that my 150cc hybrid scooter would have made any impact at the Ulster Grand Prix. My friends thought I was mad riding down the M6 on a scooter, but I enjoyed the challenge. Out of interest, on my way back from the cricket I decided to change my route and travel home via the east coast of England, riding through the Scottish border and on to Arbroath and

Jim Rea - motorbike enthusiast

eventually riding west to Stranraer. About fifty miles from Arbroath I stopped at a roadside hot food van for a cup of tea. I noticed a young man probably in his early twenties standing looking into the hedge as he drank his tea or coffee. I noticed his small motorcycle, a Honda 90. Suddenly something prompted me to go and offer him £10. I thought he might consider me mad, so I gently approached him and said, "You may find this very strange but I have just been prompted to give you £10." The guy looked at me and smiled. He then told me that he was unemployed and was on his way to Arbroath to a job interview. "I am almost out of petrol and I have no money. I am praying to God that something will turn up." I couldn't believe it. I wished him well and gave him the money with my visiting card, hoping that he would get the job.

A few weeks passed and then I got a letter from him, explaining that he was a Christian and a member of a community church in Yorkshire. He had got the job in one of Arbroath's fish processing companies. He was amazed how his prayer was answered and thanked me.

I often tried to unravel this experience. Some may consider it to be coincidental, others could suggest it was telepathy. I think it was the Holy Spirit. It taught me the lesson that when prompted to do something good, just do it. My friend certainly discovered when he prayed that day, the truth of those words written by the late Archbishop William Temple:

"When I pray, coincidences happen, and when I don't, they don't."

A POINT OF NO RETURN CHANGED IN A MOMENT

It was July 1969 and I was helping with the chaplaincy at the Royal Victoria Hospital, all part of my training for ministry. I was asked urgently to visit a young woman in the Royal Maternity Hospital. Arriving at the ward I was taken aside by a nurse. She pointed to a bed and told me that Bernadette was in early pregnancy, but had taken an overdose. I recall that as I approached her the young woman was drowsy and disorientated.

I spoke briefly to her, assuring her that the Lord loved her and that she and her baby were both greatly valued by Him. I then said a prayer. I must confess that in years to come when I had memories of this experience, which at the time I found very daunting, I wondered if in my inexperience I had said the right thing.

Over forty years have passed. It is the 11th July 2011 and we are having a day of prayer in the Shankill Methodist Church, an initiative launched by Brother David Jardine and the Divine Healing Ministries. These were trying years with the nearby parading protest at Ardoyne, and so many other flash points throughout the province. Over many years David Jardine had called for special days of

Old Shankill Church

prayer, encouraging people from all religious backgrounds to come together. For years we gathered on 11th July to pray for a peaceful day of parading on the 12th. The often peaceful outcome always amazed me.

As the event ended, a woman called me aside and asked if I could give her a few minutes of my time. She explained that in her early twenties, she had been in an extremely abusive relationship. Having moved out of that relationship she ended up being cared for by the Salvation Army. She was in early pregnancy when she saw no future for her or her child. She was at a point of no return and decided to take an overdose, with all the possibilities of aborting the child. In critical condition she was taken to the Royal Maternity Hospital. There a young minister had come to see her to pray, and she heard him say, "For God has not given us a spirit of fear, but of power, and love and of a sound mind."

Shankill Road Methodist Church

I have no recollection of sharing those words from St Paul's letter to Timothy with her, but somehow she did remember them and it had made a difference, because on that July day Bernadette was involved in the Prayer Ministry of Divine Healing Ministries with Brother David Jardine and is an active member of a Christian Fellowship. She told me she always remembered my name, and one day in a counselling situation the counsellor suggested she should try to find me to tell me this story. She rejoiced that she gave birth to her son in January 1970. He was now in his forties and doing well.

I did nothing special that day in 1969, only what any pastor would do in a similar situation. But meeting Bernadette in 2011 and being in touch with her since has convinced me how special a person she is. More than anything else is her amazing faith in Jesus Christ and her efforts to encourage others who have travelled on her journey, to discover there is One who can bring freedom from fear, to experience His power and love and a sound mind.

SALVATION ARMY AND THE HOMELESS

One of the beneficiaries from the sale of this book will be the the Salvation Army for their work amongst the homeless, along with the Welcome Centre and Hosford House.

From my early days in the ministry I would sometimes seek the help of the Salvation Army for a homeless person. Trying to learn the history of this work in Northern Ireland, I discovered that it began in Belfast in 1905 with humble beginnings in a house on the Malone Road. This was the Army's response to the many homeless and destitute people in the city in the early 20th century.

It all stemmed from the revolutionary preaching and teaching of William Booth, a former Nottingham pawnbroker, who became a minister of a branch of the Methodist Church. He and his wife Catherine left because they saw that the focus of their ministry was to be the bringing of the gospel to the poorest of the poor. It was in 1865 in London that Booth founded the Salvation Army, which is now working in 128 countries.

The Army, motivated by its Christian faith, offers practical support and services to all who need them, regardless of ethnicity, religion, gender or sexual

William Booth

orientation. The work includes campaigning and influencing social policy, alongside the provision of services for those suffering as a result of homelessness, modern slavery, poverty, addiction, ageism, debt, unemployment and isolation.

Salvation Army Hostel Belfast

The most prominent homeless centre here is Centenary House, fondly known as "the Waring Street Hostel", which together with the adjoining Calder Fountain building provides for homeless men (and lately women) and men on release from prison, and contains the city's Emergency Night Shelter for those in need of emergency accommodation. Over 80 people are accommodated there nightly. A sign of the changing times is the replacement of the name "hostel" with "lifehouse."

In 2016 the Salvation Army launched another project for homeless families on Belfast's Grosvenor Road, and this has helped several hundred people.

The Army's slogan 'Heart to God and Hand to Man' remains their firm focus in all they do. The words of General Booth are as relevant today as they were over 150 years ago:

"While women weep, I'll fight.
While little children go hungry as they do now, I'll fight.
While men go to prison, in and out, in and out as they do now, I'll fight.
While there is a drunkard left,
while there is a poor lost girl upon the streets,
while there is one dark soul without the light of God, I'll fight -
I'll fight to the very end." -

William Booth 1829-1912.

HE NEVER TOUCHED THE STUFF

If my father was ever offered an alcoholic drink, he would smile and remark that he had never tasted the stuff. As a young man he became a member of the Independent Order of Rechabites, one of the many abstinence organisations that mushroomed as a result of the drinking culture amongst the working classes in the early part of the 20th century. The Rechabites had a brass band called the Rescue Tent. My father was a keen musician so, having signed the abstinence pledge, he joined the band.

I couldn't claim that I had never touched the stuff. In my early teens I heard many sermons suggesting that when Jesus turned the water into wine, it wasn't alcoholic. I wasn't at all convinced and had an occasional drink, but I did see that Scripture warned against the perils of drunkenness and that sometimes by our example we could cause others to stumble.

While my father didn't drink, several members of my mother's family were heavy boozers, I guess addicted. As hardworking men they would drink at the weekends, stagger home and often act foolishly. As the saying goes, "When drink goes in, wit goes out." So from my early experiences I saw no big issue in becoming a total abstainer. However I have never seen abstinence as one of the necessities in order get to heaven.

During my life as a minister I became highly aware of our drinking culture, and in recent years, the incredible availability of drugs. I have conducted many funerals where death has been due to the use of alcohol or drugs. Recent figures show

I. O. R. Rescue Tent Brass Band.

that over three hundred people die in Northern Ireland each year as a direct use of alcohol alone, and these do not include many other related deaths such as suicide and road accidents where alcohol or drugs are a factor. A recent major report has looked at alcohol's damage to the brain, now called ARBD, Alcohol Related Brain Damage. The report is alarming.

In the early 1990s working in east Belfast, I became concerned about people with an addiction and its relationship to homelessness. This led to the creation of Hosford House by the East Belfast Mission.

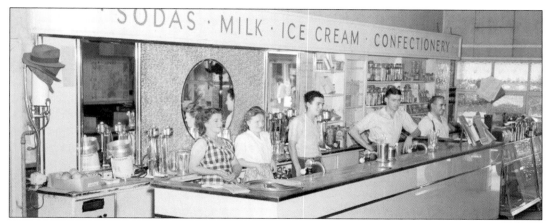

Typical 'Milk Bar / Cafe' a once popular alternative to regular bars

A few years ago I was asked to join the board of the Irish Temperance League, an organisation created in Belfast in 1837. Some of the better known names associated with ITL's aims were J.P.Corry, Edward Harland, Forster Green and Dr. Barnardo.

In the late 1880s and into the early twentieth century, ITL established coffee stands and cafés as an alternative to the 600+ pubs in Belfast. In 1877 they opened the Lombard Café and in 1943 the Kensington Hotel in the city.

In the 1970s things changed. Their cafés were no longer popular, and the troubles, particularly around central Belfast, resulted in the sale of all the property. A major plus was that this produced a substantial investment fund, enabling grants to help those educating the young on the use of alcohol and drugs, and to other organisations with a Christian ethos who were working to help people out of addiction. Education about alcohol and

The Pledge

drugs has never been more needed, and the number of people needing help to beat addictions is ever increasing. Ultimately, my father would have considered the ability to overcome the craving for drink as the outcome of a Christian faith. I never got to ask him, did he sign the pledge to join the band or did he join the band because he had signed the pledge? Whatever, I think he made a good choice.

Note: The name Rechabites comes from the Old Testament book of Jeremiah.
They lived in tents and abstained from alcohol.

"We will drink no wine, for Jonadab the son of Rechab, our father, commanded us, saying 'You shall drink no wine, you nor your sons, forever. You shall not build a house, sow seed, plant a vineyard, nor have any of these; but all your days you shall dwell in tents, that you may live many days in the land where you are sojourners.'" Jeremiah 35:6

GETTING THE ADDRESS RIGHT

Omeath Street

Billy was a one-off, like so many others who came to the East Belfast Mission in the 1990s. It was obvious from what he said that he had issues in his former life and had battled a drink problem. He also had a bad fall, causing him a disability which included not only a mobility problem but slurred and halting speech. He would close an eye and point to draw your attention. One might have thought he was drunk, but he certainly wasn't. Out of his difficult past Billy had turned to Christ, and this for him was life-transforming.

He was a popular figure in the Mission and came regularly to our midweek prayer meeting where he also liked to pray. His prayers would never have made it into the Book of Common Prayer as they were not always liturgically correct, but they were certainly original. He always prayed for people by name and sometimes offered more information than was necessary.

One night as he was praying he mentioned a lady called Sadie who lived at 36 Omeath Street, going into some details about her illness. Time passed and some others prayed, then there was a lull. Suddenly I heard Billy's voice. Slowly it came, "Lord, my apology, I'm sorry, Sadie lives in 42 Omeath Street." I heard some chuckles in the meeting and there were some hands over mouths to stop people laughing out loud. This story was often told.

Billy

I often think of Billy's prayer. Despite the humorous nature of it, I believe God heard it. I recall that the early disciples mustn't have felt they were very good at prayer because they asked Jesus to teach them to pray, and he gave them the perfect pattern for prayer in the Lord's Prayer.

I am also reminded of St Paul's words in his letter to the Romans: "In the same way, the Spirit helps us in our weakness. We do not know what we ought to pray for, but the Spirit himself intercedes for us through wordless groans. And he who searches our hearts knows the mind of the Spirit, because the Spirit intercedes for God's people in accordance with the will of God." Romans 8:26-27

In the book of Hebrews the writer informs us about a God who understands all human weakness, sympathises with us and treats us with mercy as he presents our petitions to the Throne of Grace: Jesus our great High Priest and Mediator (Hebrews 4:15).

After I left east Belfast I heard that Billy was terminally ill. I called to see him at the hospice. Now weak, he characteristically closed one eye and pointed his finger upwards. He had no words this time, but I knew the address where Billy was going and he didn't have to apologise.

SAM AND GERRY

'Quiet Peacemakers' is what artist Susan Hughes called her exhibition in 2014 to honour those who in a quiet way contributed to peace in Northern Ireland. Sam and Gerry take their place with over thirty others. The Reverend Sam Burch is a Methodist minister I have known for over fifty years. Father Gerry Reynolds was, until his death in 2015, a Redemptorist priest at Clonard Monastery.

Sam Burch had been the minister in several Methodist churches, but in 1985 he felt led to become the full time worker and leader at the Cornerstone Community. Sir Cyril Black, a leading Baptist evangelical, had bought two semi-detached houses on the Springfield Road close to the peace wall. The group took its name from the words of St Paul in Ephesians 2:19-20 describing Christians as members of God's household in which Jesus Christ is the chief cornerstone. The aim was 'To give witness that people from different religious traditions could live and work for peace in Northern Ireland'. All of this was centralised in a prayer ministry. People from different Christian backgrounds and from all parts of the world came to live and often study at Cornerstone. It was not always a comfortable place to be, with many nights of violence nearby. The heroic Sam Burch went on undaunted but virtually unnoticed.

Artist Susan Hughes and Belfast Lord Mayor Nichola Mallon

In 1990 Sam rang me and asked if I would be willing to join with some other ministers to meet leading members of the Republican movement. My immediate response was somewhat guarded. I was concerned that, living in east Belfast, if it became known I was in talks with spokespersons for the IRA, it could put me and my family at risk, but I agreed.

Sam Burch had become a close friend of Father Gerry Reynolds and he explained to me that the purpose of these conversations was to help Sinn Féin understand the fears of

Clonard Monastery

people living in broadly unionist loyalist communities. At this time it was our understanding that politicians from north and south would not entertain talks with Sinn Féin.

I still recall my first meeting in Clonard with Gerry Adams and two others. The meetings were civil but occasionally confrontational. Adams always listened respectfully and agreed that the content of conversations would be confidential. In fairness, nothing was ever leaked. Sam sought to facilitate the conversation,

Father Gerry Reynolds and Sam Burch

alongside the better known Father Alex Reid. On one occasion Gerry Adams passed me a mug of tea. "I think that's yours, Jim." It was a surreal moment.

The meetings involving me and some others ultimately faded out. At the time it was hard to know who was meeting whom. New players were in the field and the significant Hume/Adams talks began in 1993. For me these conversations were valuable as they opened other doors in the days to come.

Sam and Gerry Reynolds had a passion to bring comfort to people who had become victims of the troubles. In 1986 Sam escorted Gerry to the home of Dennis Taggart, the UDR man who had been shot dead by the IRA when he was getting out of his car in the Shankill Road. Both men prayed with his mother Peggy, who embraced Gerry and said, "I'm glad you came." Gerry gave her a carving of Jesus in tears which permanently hung on the wall of her home.

This experience brought about visits to around 50 families on each side of the peace line who had been affected by the troubles. Sam records, "We go there and just experience the first-hand shock and pain.... to feel the hurt, to see some healing taking place." Gerry records how after the Shankill bomb he went the next day and cried with the bereaved families.

The days leading up to Easter 1988 in Northern Ireland were horrific. At Milltown Cemetery during the funerals of three IRA members killed in Gibraltar, a Loyalist gunman, Michael Stone, launched a grenade and gun attack on the mourners. Three people were killed and fifty were injured. Three days later during the funeral of Kevin Brady, who was killed in the Milltown attack, two army corporals, Derek Wood and David Howers, who had driven into the area were brutally attacked and shot dead.

Good Friday was now only a few days away and there was a peace march scheduled. The idea was to march from Clonard on the Falls Road to Woodvale Park in Protestant west Belfast, but it was considered by some, including the police, as ill-advised. As the sun shone that afternoon 1500 people turned up and took two hours to go through the narrow gate on the peace wall.

As the crowd carrying the cross and singing hymns came up the Shankill Road, they were attacked by a few young men. I recall one shouting "Enniskillen" as he lunged into the crowd, only to be arrested. A young woman reacted by dropping to her knees on the road to pray. Then suddenly the rain came in torrents and drenched the crowd. As we reached Woodvale Park, Sam Burch addressed the crowd, and then something remarkable happened, something I'd never seen before in my life: a stunning triple rainbow appeared in the sky. Calls of 'amen' and 'praise the Lord' could be heard in the crowd. Gerry and Sam saw it as God's blessing on the day.

When it was all over Sam and Gerry rang the police insisting that no charges be brought against the young men who attacked the march.

On the 30th November 2015 Gerry's life on earth ended, but Sam, an unsung hero and quiet peacemaker now in his early 90s, presses on.

For me Sam and Gerry emulated the words of Stuart Townsend and Keith Getty's well-known hymn;

In Christ alone my hope is found,
He is my light, my strength, my song;
This Cornerstone, this solid Ground,
Firm through the fiercest drought and storm.
What heights of love, what depths of peace,
When fears are stilled, when strivings cease!
My Comforter, my All in All,
Here in the love of Christ I stand.

THE NICEST THING IN NEW YORK

Carl Gibney

I met Carl Gibney when I went to be a minister in Irvinestown, County Fermanagh. Carl was a highly educated medical practitioner, who changed to dentistry. In Fermanagh dentists were scarce and Carl's role was highly valuable.

He was brought up in Oldcastle, Co Meath. Relatively new to Irvinestown like ourselves, Carl and his wife Marie would soon become our lifelong friends. Carl was a thinker. He would often ask big questions challenging his own religious background. He showed an interest in people from every political and religious background and tradition. He was totally opposed to violence and would be outspoken against his co-religionists if they gave any hint of supporting terrorism. The troubles in Northern Ireland hurt him deeply. Eventually he decided to return to work close to his home place in Kells, County Meath.

Carl was from a different religious tradition to me, and I recall discussing many aspects of the Christian faith with him. He always wanted to cut through the tradition of doctrines that had to be accepted because they had been handed down. For Carl faith had be authentic, not just something you had been told to believe.

Despite his success in his dental practice in Kells he gave little attention to wealth and prosperity. He had a great quest for learning. Some time before he died we had a conversation about quantum physics - it was double-Dutch to me!

Carl was a fascinated observer of life. After a visit he and Marie made to New York I asked how he had found this fascinating city, as I shared my own memories of being there. After telling me of their visits to some significant landmarks in the city, he looked at me and said, "Well, you would know Marie likes the shops, I'm not so interested. So one day as she was browsing I sat on a seat on the pavement and watched the world go by." He went on to recall that he could not help noticing a very attractive young woman immaculately dressed in a business suit. She was lingering and looking about her. Then to Carl's surprise she went up and queued at a hot food van. Carl was a bit startled and thought to himself that a burger and fries was a strange kind of dish for this lady. He kept watching as she took the meal and walked towards a man who was begging, then she kneeled down on the street and handed it to him. "That was the nicest thing I saw in New York." As he spoke I thought of the words of Jesus, "Inasmuch as you did it to one of the least of these my brethren, you did it to me."

Another day as we looked out of his front window in Kells, we were watching people walking on the street outside. Then Carl pointed and said, "Jim, look out there, not one of those people will be here in one hundred years. Life is short and we must use it well."

Carl Gibney got his priorities right. He ultimately found a faith centred in Jesus Christ, and I had the honour of sharing in his funeral service. Some words written in the Irish Times after his death in 2019 summed him up: "Carl walked into the valley of the shadow of death, feeling the comfort of the Lord on his final journey." And I am sure the comfort of the Lord on his final journey was much more wonderful than the experience at the hot food van in New York.

MEMORIES ARE MADE OF THIS

Dean Martin

While the title suggests the famous song by the late Dean Martin, looking back on life there are memories that don't fade. Some are already to be found in earlier stories that I have written. However, the eleven years before I retired were eventful.

I recall the days Carol and I spent in Portadown and the welcome we received by a deeply committed leadership. Some experiences remain ingrained in my memory. In 1999 Drumcree had brought great problems to the town. When I arrived I suggested in the light of the impasse that the seven Methodist congregations should come together to pray. Much to my encouragement over fifty people arrived on the next Wednesday and prayed for a peaceful resolution to the impasse. This special summer prayer meeting continues to the present day and the town is a better place.

One Portadown man, Billy McCrory, was a very friendly character but told me that the message of the gospel never quite got through to him. On the 5th of January 2003 in Thomas Street, as the Methodist Covenant Service was underway, Billy seemed very upset and was shaking. Then he stood up and spoke out a few words, declaring that he had been touched by the Holy Spirit and had now surrendered his life to Christ. This was the stuff of the 18th century Methodist revival! Billy was one of a number of people, young and old, who made this discovery of new life in Christ. This remains Billy's testimony as he continues to serve the Lord.

On a lighter note is my interest in football. I adopted Portadown F.C. as my club, with divided loyalties when they played Cliftonville. The ever-dependable Steven Wright suggested to Ronnie McFaul, the Portadown manager, that I should be chaplain at the club. Ronnie readily agreed and I

Thomas Street Methodist Church

enjoyed every minute of it, meeting players and spectators and sometimes offering them pastoral support.

Eddie Drury was a postman who raised many thousands of pounds for charities, including the Southern Area Hospice in Newry. He was also on the board of Glenavon Football Club. He had previously been a member of a loyalist flute band. Early in my time at Thomas Street Eddie became a Christian. He had wonderful community spirit, reaching across all divides, and had a love for the poor and homeless. He became part of a Christian group, the Band of Brothers, former loyalist band members who share their Christian experience with bandsmen and spectators at parades. Eddie was awarded an MBE for his charitable work.

That reminds me of another MBE, the unforgettable and respected Elizabeth Forbes. Elizabeth was a great encourager and was similarly honoured for her amazing work in Thomas Street Girls' Brigade Company.

In 2003 when I was President of the Methodist Church I had a heart attack. Amazingly, having had six stents inserted, within a few weeks I was back at work. In 2006 I was stationed to Shankill Methodist Church, an unusual thing in Methodism as it was our home church. On our arrival, memories flooded back. I had left school at fifteen without any formal qualifications. I was seventeen when the Rev Harold Good, a final year student at Edgehill College, showed our youth group at Shankill a slide show of what it was like to be a student at the college. In the moment I thought, I would like to go there someday. It proved to be significant.

I recall affectionately the Rev Charlie Keys, a pastor par excellence who in 1967 brought my name forward, together with that of my close friend Kenneth Irvine, as recommended candidates for the Methodist ministry and of the Rev Sydney Callaghan who more than anyone was our encourager and mentor. Memories of the day Carol and I were married on June 20th 1970; ironically it was on Sunday 20th of June 2010, forty years later, that I retired. One of the 'oldies' Norman Coates was still there in the congregation. He remained as always the effervescent encourager from those early days until his death in 2019 aged 96.

In June 2006 I developed myasthenia gravis and became badly inhibited in my ability to work, due to muscle weakness and slurred speech and swallowing issues. This was followed in June 2008 by a crisis requiring hospital admission. One day in the hospital I was very unwell. Feeling hopeless, I looked up and saw a small bird land on the windowsill. It was a significant moment, because my mind was suddenly taken back to my installation as President of the Methodist Church, when my friend the outstanding West Indian singer Clover Watts sang, "His eye is on the sparrow and I know He watches you." It brought me through a dark moment to a better day.

And so I press on, still helping around the Shankill.

Note: The Methodist Covenant Service dates back to John Wesley and generally takes place on the first Sunday in January, where members are encouraged to reflect on their lives and renew their commitment to Christ, and to share the outcome with others.

STRANGER IN THE NIGHT

The first time I met Billy Waite was in 2006 in the congregation of Woodvale Methodist Church. Billy was physically a big man, a widower who had a large family. I discovered he was a country man who lived some miles from the church, at Dundrod near to the home of the Ulster Grand Prix. My first real contact with him came after the sad death of his daughter Jean, who lived with him. Billy was now living alone, with some family support.

Ulster Grand Prix

On a visit a few days after Jean's funeral, I offered Billy a small booklet which he graciously declined, informing me that he could not read. Then he told me his story. He had grown up in the 1930s on the Old Lodge Road, a very poor area of Belfast. At eight years old he began to work to help his poor family cope. He told me he was a champion school truant, going in the front door of the school and then out the back door. In order to avoid school he would do all sorts of messages for local shops, including delivering newspapers to earn a little money.

Despite his reading deficiency he was an intelligent man. He went on to tell me that he had worked hard throughout his life and had made a good living, doing heavy labouring work for animal feed mills. Heavy drinking used to be part of his lifestyle and he would consume a ten-glass bottle of whiskey just about every day. He went on to explain how over twenty years before, his wife Maureen had become seriously ill. She was a woman of deep Christian faith. The realisation of her terminal illness troubled him greatly, but it didn't change his lifestyle. In fact whiskey helped him escape from reality.

One very dark night on the 2nd March 1992 the wind was howling, it was cold and there was heavy rain. There was a knock at the door, and outside stood a man wrapped up well in an overcoat and scarf. He asked Billy if he would allow him to pray with Maureen. Having prayed, the stranger turned to Billy and asked him if would like to give his life to Christ. To the amazement of Maureen, Billy prayed for forgiveness and trusted Christ as his Lord and Saviour.

Maureen died in November 1992, but by now Billy's life was transformed. He had experienced the truth of St Paul's words, "Therefore, if anyone is in Christ, the new creation has come: the old has gone, the new is here!" (2 Corinthians 5:17).

At Ballydonaghy Road Dundrod, Billy fulfilled a desire of his late wife Maureen, as there now stands a Mission Hall on ground donated by Billy. This is only part of his legacy. He has left behind a large family of children and grandchildren, many of whom have followed his example and make a great contribution to the fellowship of Woodvale Methodist Church.

Who was the man who led Billy to Christ on March 2nd 1992? Billy could never recall his name. The visitor disappeared quietly that night and to his knowledge Billy Waite never met him again.

He was God's stranger in the night.

Ballydonaghy Mission Hall

THE MAN WHO SAID "NO" TO THE SERBIAN DICTATOR

I still recall the cold evening in the early 1990s, when I received a phone call from my friend and local Presbyterian minister, the Rev Victor Ryan. He asked if I would see a man he thought I may be able to help. When the man arrived I guessed he was in his late 20s. Initially I thought he might have wanted money, but immediately he opened his wallet showing me that he had thirty five pounds. He explained that he was from Macedonia once part of the old Yugoslavia. With fear all over his face he informed me that he was being enlisted into the Serbian Army by Slobodan Milošević, who is now imprisoned as a war criminal from a conflict that caused the deaths of around 140,000 people.

Slobodan Milošević

My friend couldn't support this awful war. Explaining that it was brother against brother, he compared Milošević to Hitler. He had decided to escape his country and was smuggled onto a fishing boat which landed in Galway. He'd been in Northern Ireland for several months, making a living by calling at homes offering to do odd jobs, mostly gardening. He then explained that he had been living in an old abandoned car but now, in winter, things were getting tough. The trouble was he was illegal in the UK. I agreed that we would give him accommodation in our homeless unit at Hosford House. Hearing his forename I realised it might be somewhat unpronounceable for some of the locals. Humorously, I told him that we would call him Sammy and he was to reveal his background to no one.

Serbian Army

For the next number of months we looked after him. He proved to be a great asset doing all sorts of voluntary work and getting on well with the residents of Hosford House. He attended church regularly and though the congregation knew little about him, typically they welcomed him. However I was at odds as to what I should do. This situation could not go on interminably.

One day it dawned on me that he had entered Ireland from the Irish Republic. I thought of my friend Gordon Wilson, then a Senator in the Irish Government. Quickly a discreet meeting with Gordon, Sammy and myself was arranged in a city centre cafe. Gordon said that he had good contacts with the Irish Foreign Affairs Department. I was never sure what ultimately happened but one day Sammy went to Dublin only to call me and tell me he had got the necessary papers to live in the Republic. Under EU rules he could now move to Northern Ireland. Soon after, a man who owned an electronics company in Lisburn rang me to see I could recommend any reliable people to work for him. I suggested Sammy and several weeks later he rang me again to thank for getting him someone so gifted and reliable.

Sammy went to live around Lisburn but on the following Christmas Day, to my surprise, there he was sitting in the balcony of the East Belfast Mission. When the service ended, he came rushing down the aisle of the church and asked me if he could address the congregation.

"This is who I really am," he explained to them, "I am from Macedonia, and today I should be dead, as I was to be enlisted into the Serbian Army by Milošević. Turning to me he said, "You saved my life,"and presented me with a cake and a bottle of wine from Macedonia (he mustn't have known that I was TT). People were moved to tears and then there was applause.

Soon after, I lost contact with him, but the last thing I heard, was that he was manager in one of our well known supermarkets. I often think about him, pray for him and wonder where he is. Wherever I hope he is doing well.

PRAYER CHANGES THINGS

The Reverend Brother David Jardine is a Church of Ireland minister, who since 1973 has been a member of the Anglican Society of St Francis. Best known as Brother David, he has taken three demanding vows that most of us would shy away from: poverty, chastity and obedience. He maintains obedience to be the most difficult. I have known David for well over thirty years. He hails from Banbridge and is an only son who sadly lost his father when he was only nineteen. A capable sportsman, he's played cricket for Queen's and the YMCA. He felt the call to ministry and after studying at Queen's he went to the Church of Ireland training college for clergy in Dublin.

I first heard about David in the early 1980s, when ministering in east Belfast. People in their mid years spoke of the wonderful influence he had upon them as young people, and the pastoral care he gave to their parents when a curate in St Patrick's Church of Ireland on the Newtownards Road. As a Franciscan brother, David owns nothing, not that he does not have basic provisions, but he has sacrificed everything to live a simple life of prayer. He spends many hours each day praying and interceding for people with a variety of needs. David spent some years as a Prison Chaplain in Crumlin Road jail. He led many of the inmates to Christ and had an incredible influence on Packy Hamilton an ex-paramilitary who has had an amazing ministry and wrote the book, 'A Cause Worth Living For.'

'Packy' Hamilton

Many will know Brother David primarily through his work with Divine Healing Ministries. For years through the troubles he gathered people from all over the province to pray, often for whole days of prayer when trouble was likely. Things often changed for the better, and he has witnessed men from republican and loyalist backgrounds reconciled, emphasising the need to be forgiven and to forgive.

Now in his late seventies, against some negative advice he has pioneered a Christian-based project called 'Equipping for Life'. This provided one-to-one tuition in schools for young people in areas where education is undervalued. The interest and uptake are amazing.

Recently I asked David what was central to his life to which he replied:

"No situation is beyond transformation when we bring it before God in prayer."

I seriously reflected on this comment. Is this true for someone like me who is often a doubter and expects the worst-case scenario? My experience, however, suggests that God does change things, though not always in the way we want. My grandmother

Brother David Jardine

lived through two wars, the hungry 1930s and four years of the troubles in relative poverty. I can still hear her say, "God never gives you a hard road to walk without giving you a decent pair of shoes to walk on it," which resonates with what David said.

As Brother David also often says,

"Wherever you are, whatever your circumstances,
God is never more than a prayer away."

He is completely committed to Jesus Christ and remains one of the most impressive Christians that I have ever met.

FOOTPRINTS IN THE AFGHAN DESERT

My phone rang one day in September 2007. The caller asked if I would be willing to have Margaret Fishback Powers to speak at Shankill Methodist Church where I was minister. The name meant nothing to me and the caller seemed surprised. "She's famous!" he exclaimed. "Margaret is the author of 'Footprints in the Sand'." I immediately realised who she was. I was familiar with the poem; I had seen it in numerous places on plaques and inspirational cards, in gift shops and in many of the homes of people I visited. Many had found solace from it through difficult situations, but I was totally unaware of the author's name.

Jim with Margaret Fishback Powers

I was pleased to have Margaret and her husband Paul to come to the church to speak. She recounted how in 1963 she had a dream and the words came to her, explaining how the poem is based on Christian beliefs and describes life as a person walking on a beach with God, leaving two sets of footprints in the sand. Sometimes the two footprints merge into one, and this happens especially at the lowest and most hopeless moments of the person's life. The person thinks God has abandoned them, but God explains that it was during their times of trial and suffering, when they could only see only one set of footprints, that God was in fact carrying them.

In her book 'Footprints in the Sand,' Margie, as she is better known, tells numerous stories about people who in the darkest moments of their lives found hope and inspiration from the poem.

One day a few years ago I conducted a funeral in a small house in north Belfast where an elderly lady, a much loved grandmother, had died. Her grandson, a young man in his twenties, asked if he could say a few words. He seemed somewhat nervous but I agreed to let him speak. When his time came, he lifted a small framed card of 'Footprints' from beside the television, explaining that he wanted to read it, and that he had served on two tours with the British Army in Afghanistan. Holding it up he said, "This was my granny's prayer for me." He had kept it in the breast pocket of his uniform and read it every day.

I then explained how the author had been to our church on the Shankill Road a few years earlier to tell her story. This time instead of the stories I had read about 'Footprints,' this was a face to face encounter with a young man who found hope in the darkest and most dangerous days of his life, in the deserts of Afghanistan.

Footprints
Also Known As "I Had a Dream"

One night I dreamed a dream.
I was walking along the beach with my Lord.
Across the dark sky flashed scenes from my life.
For each scene, I noticed two sets of footprints in the sand,
one belonging to me and one to my Lord.

When the last scene of my life shot before me
I looked back at the footprints in the sand.
There was only one set of footprints.
I realised that this was at the lowest and saddest times of my life.
This always bothered me and I questioned the Lord about my dilemma.

"Lord, You told me when I decided to follow You,
You would walk and talk with me all the way.
But I'm aware that during the most troublesome times of my life
there is only one set of footprints. I just don't understand why,
when I need You most, You leave me."

He whispered, "My precious child, I love you and will never leave you,
never, ever, during your trials and testings.
When you saw only one set of footprints, It was then that I carried you."

Margaret Fishback Powers, 1964

IN THE SOUP

Grand Central Hotel Belfast 1940s

When I was a young lad, my mother would wave her finger and quote a text from the Old Testament book of Numbers, "Be sure your sin will find you out." It was to warn me that if I had been guilty of any misdemeanour it would come to light. I can still see her finger waving at me as she repeated this verse.

I often reminded my dad of my mother's words when he held court and dined out on the following story.

My father served his apprenticeship as a sheet metal worker with the firm Gambles in south Belfast. He told many stories about his early experiences. I guess the funniest is about the day he went to work at the Grand Central Hotel in Belfast. Before going into decline this was one of the city's top hotels, and in the 1940s and 50s it catered for the great and the good who

could afford to dine or stay there. Now its name has re-emerged in a new location as one of Belfast's poshest hotels. My father describes being assigned to a big job on the kitchen's ventilating system with his journeyman Jackie Barr. They had to work overnight as the kitchen needed to be in full use during the day.

They were up sorting the ventilators with my father working on a ladder when, as he would later tell graphically, he slipped and landed in large of pot of tomato soup. He describes the soup being in his socks and boots and all over the bottom of his overalls. Believing the pot of soup had been left over from the day before, he quickly got himself together and tipped the residue of the soup from his shoes back into the pot, and squeezed out his socks over the pot. As best he could, he made himself respectable and continued working.

At around 6.00am the chef arrived, looked around the kitchen and admired the work that had gone on overnight. "Well done, lads!" he remarked. Then, pleased with what he had seen, he offered Jackie and Billy some breakfast. My father asked if the soup was for throwing out. "Oh no!" said the chef, "it's on the first course for today's special lunch with Lord Glentoran and the Privy Council."

My dad said nothing. But he often told the story and got a laugh. With a twinkle in his eyes he maintained that he listened to the news to see if there were any casualties, but he heard nothing more, so he thought my mother's Bible text hadn't applied this time, "be sure your sin will find you out." Maybe more like a well known saying,

The New Grand Central Hotel Belfast

"What you don't know won't do you any harm." Perhaps on this occasion, discretion was the better part of valour.

TWO SPORTING EVENTS WITH SAD MEMORIES

I still recall the 2nd of March 1974 when my friend Douglas Hudson and I made our way from Irvinestown, County Fermanagh to Lansdowne Road, Dublin, to watch Ireland play Scotland. Douglas was a great rugby fan, and the deal was that if I took the car he bought the tickets. On this occasion Douglas informed me that we were taking two passengers. On our way through Enniskillen we picked up John and his 10-year-old son Paul. Never having met them before, I found they proved to be very good company. The young lad was so pleasant and well-mannered.

Lord Louis Mountbatten and crew

The game was thrilling as Ireland won 9.6 (under the old scoring methods). What was particularly exciting was that Scotland in the dying seconds could have drawn the game with a penalty in front of the posts, but the Scottish players decided to run the ball with the hope of getting it to the line, scoring a try, and winning the game. They failed, but as the whistle blew, this sporting gesture was applauded by the Irish fans.

On our way home the little boy was full of excitement at the outcome of the game. I guess it may have been his first experience of international rugby at Lansdowne Road. On the way home, I asked him about his interests, and how he was doing at school. He was a really nice lad, and I stopped the car at Kells in County Meath, went into a shop and presented him with some sweets. His face lit up as he tucked into the bag of goodies.

Over six years have now passed and it's the 27th August 1979. As a cricket fan I was at Downpatrick enjoying the last game of the season. But you will understand why I can remember little about who was playing or the result, as on leaving the ground, news was coming through of an explosion at Mullaghmore in County Sligo. I knew this part of the world well: when I lived in Fermanagh it was often a place for a day out. Soon we were to hear that Lord Louis Mountbatten had been killed in an act of terrorism; the Dowager Baroness Brabourne, their grandson and a boy helping on the boat were also casualties.

In August 2019 forty years have passed and there was a memorial service at Mullaghmore which included a visit from Prince Charles. His words of reconciliation were both emotional and powerful. Later I watched a television interview with the mother of the boy who had been helping on the boat. It was deeply moving and I will never forget her bravery. The impact of her deep loss she described to the Irish

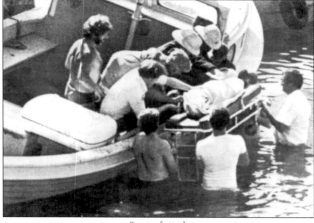
Scene of attack

News: "It still remains with me. I felt the forgiveness in the church and the feeling of warmth and generosity, and extending the hand to others and sort of nearly giving them a hug. It was palpable and it was just a marvellous experience." She spoke of the singing of school children, including Bethany McLoughlin (17), whose grandfather Gerard McKinney was among the 13 Bloody Sunday victims. The tearful mother said that the day's events had been a significant step in her own healing process.

What she probably did not know was that I had bought sweets for her son Paul Maxwell on the way back from a rugby match in Dublin when he was just 10. Watching that memorial service

Paul Maxwell

Paul's mother

on television in 2019 my thoughts are unchanged, that this was an evil act, no matter what the cause. The generosity and graciousness expressed by Prince Charles and Paul's parents on that day are embedded in my memory. The rugby match I will always remember, and the drive home with Paul and his dad. But it is all so mixed with sadness. The cricket match is a blur in the light of the events that followed.

The futility of violence. Will we ever learn?

COME IN, BUT NOT HERE

On the 7th of November 2019 I attended a memorial service for a man I had never personally met, but I had heard him preach on several occasions. Professor David Gooding was a world-renowned scholar and professor of Greek at Queen's University. He was a member of the Christian Brethren, but had a ministry far and beyond that denomination. As a preacher and Bible teacher he was quite outstanding.

Professor David Gooding

Looking down from the balcony of the Crescent Church on that November evening I wasn't at all surprised when I noticed a fellow Methodist minister David Clements in the congregation. I know David well. He started his working career training to be a medical doctor. His father Billy, a friend of mine, was a reserve policeman who sadly was murdered by the IRA at Ballygawley in December 1985. It had a remarkable impact on his son David. Having completed his medical training David now felt his calling to be in the ministry of the Methodist Church.

David Clements recalls that back in the 1980s, at the end of his first year as a medical student at Queen's University, he was talking to a friend who was in his final year. "Have you any regrets?" he asked. "I could have learnt more from some of the great Christians about this place," was the reply. "Like who?" "Professor David Gooding would be top of the list."

One day David Clements found out where the Greek Department was and climbed up the stairs and knocked on the door with the name Gooding on it. "Come in," said a clear voice, and as he opened the door and went in, a very distinguished looking man peered over the top of his glasses at him and smiled. "Sir," my friend said a little nervously, "my name is Dave Clements. Is there any possibility that I could do some Bible study with you?"

Dr Gooding invited David to take a seat. "Are you a preacher, dear boy?" Then plans were made to study John's Gospel on Sunday afternoons in the summer term at Professor Gooding's house. David's suggestion of bringing some friends along was

Rev Dr David Clements

readily agreed to, and he maintains that those Sunday afternoon sessions in the lounge at Myrtlefield Park changed his life. "I have many happy memories of subsequent visits there. One in particular (a regular occurrence) is standing in the kitchen, tea in a fine bone china cup in one hand, a thick wedge of cake in the other and the two of us laughing so loudly that the neighbours must have been able to hear!"

He recalls how many Christian men and women have had a positive and significant influence on his life, but probably none had greater influence on him than David Gooding. He told me that in the years following his father's tragic death, David Gooding became a spiritual father and mentor to him. David Clements, the preacher in a different tradition of the Christian church, is still sharing the things he learnt from David Gooding. At the time he recalled that he probably did not fully realise how generous he was with his time and energy. What is unforgettable was the clarity with which Prof. Gooding taught the Bible. David Clements admits that he greatly misses those visits to Myrtlefield Park but rejoices in the Christian hope of eternal life that they both shared.

Professor John Lennox, who gave a tribute to David Gooding at the memorial service that I attended, said he once asked his friend what words he would like on his gravestone. In his own quirky way David Gooding exclaimed, "Not here!" On the 30th of August 2019 he heard the Lord call, "Come in!"

Professor John Lennox

A UNITED BLOW ON THE TWELFTH

In my school days if you wanted to learn music and play an instrument, the best way was to join one of Belfast's many bands. No, not necessarily a Blood & Thunder one as the majority are nowadays, but a brass or concert band, or part flute band.

This led me as a fourteen-year-old to join Belfast Military Band. It was really a brass and reed band based on the composition of a British Military Band, and now referred to as a concert band, I guess in case they are accused of being paramilitaries. Our band played in a small hall up a gateway in Tennent Street in north Belfast. You paid two shillings a week, were given an instrument along with some tuition, and soon you were on your way. This band in the 1920s and 1930s had been the

Belfast Military Band 12ᵗʰ July mid 70s

best band of this type in the country, for many years winning the championship prize at the annual Ulster Hall Competition. However, we had faded a bit but were still a force worth reckoning with. I never became a great player but gained the nickname 'Acker' after clarinettist Acker Bilk, whose 'Stranger on the Shore' was my party piece.

We were also a marching band and went out on the twelfth of July. We always got the best Orange lodges with their suits and hard hats, one being York L.O.L. - these were, as we would say, "respectable guys". They offered us £150 to take them to the Field.

One day at a band meeting someone suggested that we might extend some friendship to a band on the Falls Road called St Peter's Brass and Reed. They were a band who accompanied processions on high days and holy days organised by the Catholic churches of west Belfast. They had an interesting history, as after the Irish War of Independence many of them had joined the Free State Army as Bandsmen.

So it was agreed we invite them up. About six of them joined us and we all became friends. But then something happened. It was coming near the 12th of July - would we dare to invite these guys to march? So we put it to them, and to our surprise they agreed. We were aware that, many years before, the famous Argyle Flute Band were banned for some years by the Orange Order for fielding a Catholic flute player on the twelfth. So being wily cute, we told our guests that if asked, Seamus would be known as James and Liam would be William, and Sean of course would be John.

A young Jim Rea in his bandsman uniform

The sun shone and we had a great day; our friends got fitted out with uniforms and marched to the Field, where they were sumptuously fed at the expense of the lodge. On the return we made the seven-mile walk to north Belfast where we played the Queen at the Worshipful Master's house. Breaking up at the band hall we divided the £150. Two pounds and ten shillings each (£2.50) - a day's pay for many! We said goodbye to our guests as they made their way home to west Belfast.

A good friend who became a leading light in the Orange Order played the clarinet alongside me that day. I never heard that he mentioned this incident in any of his orations at lodge meetings, but I guess he would laugh at the memory now. Both bands have gone a long time now, but we knew something about power sharing before it was invented. Truly a big 'blow' for the twelfth!

Music has immense power to unite people. The early 1960s saw many such friendships, that sadly were not to be in the troubled years that followed.

HOMELESS - A PERSONAL STORY

"I never thought it would happen to me: homelessness. It's something that happens to men; older men maybe – people with beards and alcohol problems. Or maybe to those who have no family, or difficult families. Thinking about it now, I don't remember really giving homelessness much thought. Why would I? I was young, female, from a decent family. I was really protected by my family. I never went out. I wanted to, but my parents wouldn't let me. My dad was strict with us. No social life allowed. He had been brought up that way and he was looking after my mum. She was very ill. Looking back I had no idea what the world was really like.

"I left school and moved to Belfast. I had a cousin there who said I could stay with her. I was only sixteen. I thought I could train as a hairdresser, get my own place, and enjoy the city. It didn't work out that way. I ended up sofa surfing. I think that's a weird term, sofa surfing. Makes it sound fun. It's not. When you wake up on someone's sofa, day after day, knowing that they want to help but also want their home and sofa back, it's not good. I ended up in hostels, just going round and round in circles. I lost my mojo. I thought at one point I'd given up totally, lost it. One thing saved me though. I was determined not to go down the drugs route. That probably sounds funny to you. You're probably thinking why would you need to be determined? Well I'll tell you why. When you're vulnerable, and alone, and feeling like you really are the lowest of the low, drugs seem like an easy way out. I didn't take it though. "Instead I got lucky. My uncle introduced me to The Welcome Organisation. They helped me get my wee place. I got training on cooking and administration. I think I'm going to make it after all." *'Ciara' from Belfast*

From humble beginnings The Welcome Organisation has grown to become one of the most respected homelessness charities in Northern Ireland, providing potentially life-saving support for some of the most vulnerable people in our communities. Welcome began in 1996 as a small, community-led project set up to assist people who were street drinking. Currently the charity has four distinct services to help people affected by homelessness – a Drop-in Centre, a Street Outreach service, Crisis Accommodation for Women, and a Floating Support service.

Based on Townsend Street, the Drop-In Centre is within walking distance of Belfast city centre. Over the years it has seen hundreds of people coming through the doors to get anything from a cup of tea to advice and support on housing, addictions and mental health and more. The Street Outreach service provides on-the-ground support to people who are sleeping rough across the Greater Belfast area 17 hours a day. Members of the public can contact the Street Outreach team directly if they are concerned about someone on the streets.

Every night Welcome's Crisis Accommodation for Women provides a safe place to stay for ten of the most vulnerable women in the city – women who would otherwise potentially spend the night on the streets. One hundred people who have been homeless but are now in accommodation are supported through Welcome's Floating Support team. The team will make regular visits to ensure they have everything they need to retain their tenancies and to turn a house into a home.

For more info visit www.homelessbelfast.org
Welcome's Street Outreach service: 07894931047

With thanks to Kieran Hughes Fund Raising
and Marketing Manager at the Welcome Organisation.

THANKS & ACKNOWLEDGEMENTS

My appreciation to: Cedric Wilson, whose encouragement and amazing skills in publication have made this book possible; Martin Kenny, whose incredible ability with graphics and layout has greatly enhanced the book for the reader. Also Julia Grier, for her time and patience in proof reading and meticulous editing. Brenda Callaghan, for her advice on the construction of the stories. My good friend Bishop David McClay for writing the foreword. To Alf McCreary, Billy Kennedy, and Seamus Boyd for commending the book.

I also thank the church members and leaders of the Methodist Circuits of Cregagh, Pettigo and Irvinestown, East Belfast Mission, Portadown and Greater Shankill, where I have served as a minister, and to the ministerial colleagues and youth pastors with whom I shared ministry. Also to Myrtle Wright and Maureen Blevins, two wonderful encouragers and pastoral assistants on the Portadown Circuit.

Finally to my wife Carol who has been my greatest supporter and encourager in our fifty years of marriage. We have been greatly blessed with our children Judith, Barbara, Jonathan and their spouses Eoghan, Neil and Tammie. Our grandchildren Anna, Sam, Ross, Hope, Alistair and Freya.

All profits (after production and distribution costs) from the sale of this book will be donated to three homeless charities: the Welcome Organisation, East Belfast Mission's Hosford House, and the Salvation Army's homelessness work in Northern Ireland.

IRISH TEMPERANCE LEAGUE

In writing this book I want to acknowledge the support and encouragement of the Irish Temperance League, a Christian based organisation founded over one hundred and fifty years ago, which continues to support those in the frontline battle against drug abuse and alcoholism. Recent statistics inform us that in Northern Ireland almost three hundred deaths per year are exclusively attributed to alcohol abuse. This does not include the alarming use of illegal drugs resulting in tragic deaths. Several of the stories in this publication are about people who have overcome addiction to alcohol and drugs to find a new life in Christ. Working in ministry for over forty years I have had the privilege of seeing lives changed by the transforming power of God. This book tells some of those stories.

The Irish Temperance League regularly offers grants to organisations assisting people to overcome addictions, and also to those in the field of education. Considering the pressures of modern society I enthusiastically commend an alcohol- and drug-free lifestyle, and am pleased to enter into correspondence through my email address. I am also in contact with many organisations who can offer support to sufferers and their families.

Omid's story

'I came to Northern Ireland as an asylum seeker. I had to flee my home country because I was persecuted as a Christian and in great danger. As an asylum seeker I was given accommodation by the government while my application to become a refugee was processed. I was delighted to be granted refugee status which meant I could stay in Northern Ireland. But once I became a refugee I was given notice that by law I must leave the accommodation for asylum seekers the government had provided me; this is how I became homeless. Hosford gave me a room and the kind and friendly staff helped me to settle into Belfast and to improve my life.

EAST BELFAST MISSION
THE METHODIST CHURCH IN IRELAND

During my time at Hosford I achieved so many things and I had a wonderful time. I improved my English, I attended College and gained qualifications, I became a volunteer and helped other refugees and asylum seekers, I got a driving licence and a car, I became part of a Church Congregation, and I made friends across the city. The staff at Hosford helped me to join Street Soccer NI and through that I became part of the NI Homeless World Cup Team and represented Northern Ireland in the Homeless World Cup in Mexico. The following year I was a volunteer photographer with the team that competed in the Cardiff Homeless World Cup. These were some of the best experiences of my life. I am now in my own accommodation, I feel part of a community, and I am going through the selection process for the Fire Service. I am looking forward to the future and I hope to get married and buy my own home in the coming years.' Hosford has been working with the most vulnerable and marginalised in society for over 25 years. At the core of this is our homeless hostel, which was rebuilt in October 2012 as part of the project on the Lower Newtownards Road.

Each night we provide accommodation for 26 people (single men and women aged 17 years plus) and have a stepping stone approach of single rooms and apartments which helps people to rebuild their lives and work towards living independently. We offer 24/7 support and each resident has their own Support Worker who provides housing related support to help them to find and maintain their own home. Residents also have a chance to engage with all the other services Hosford and East Belfast Mission provide as well as help to link in with any relevant services in the area. Our hostel provides shelter and help to approximately 100 people each year.

We also provide support to people who are living independently but encountering problems and could lose their home. We aim to enable people to live independently through developing their skills and their ability to deal with problems. The service is about preventing homelessness by intervening in its causes. This project supports over 150 people each year. Hosford's Health and Welling Project aims to tackle the health and wellbeing issues faced by people who are homeless or at risk of homelessness. This project gives those involved opportunities to learn new skills, make progress in their lives, meet friends, and to be part of a community. The project offers a wide range of activities such as cooking, gardening, art, drama, and community events.

The work at Hosford is fundamentally about saving lives through the provision of accommodation and the prevention of homelessness. We support individuals to make positive changes in their lives, overcome the traumas they have experienced and help them to build a better future.

Aidan Byrne *Homelessness Service Manager*

**For more information T: 028 9046 3482
or visit the website at: www.ebm.org.uk**